OLLI Lunch 12/13/

COUNTRY

La Martie,
Neither of us is, yet both,
both are, picked up
in the sounds of the
time, formed by the
notes, here annotated
with some vulgar
words, stretching
creations commentary
on the music and
men, too much, too
little.

Romain

COUNTRY

The Biggest Music in America

NICK TOSCHES

A Delta Special

A Delta Special

Published by Dell Publishing Co., Inc.
1 Dag Hammarskjold Plaza
New York, New York 10017

Copyright © 1977 by Nick Tosches

Delta ® TM 755118, Dell Publishing Co., Inc.

ISBN: 0-440-51440-1

Manufactured in the United States of America

First Delta printing—April 1979

Design and typography by Giorgetta Bell McRee

TO LOUISE
with hot sauce

"Thanks"

To those who gave important data, photographs, and tapes: Cliff Bruner, Ted Daffan, Al Dexter, Doug Green, Roy Horton, George Jones, Rich Kienzle, Len Kunstadt, Bill Malone, Jim O'Neal, Bob Pinson, Tony Russell, Charlie Ryan, Malcolm Temple, Clark Thomas, Glenn White, and Charlyn Zlotnik.

To the staffs of the Country Music Foundation in Nashville, the John Edwards Memorial Foundation in Los Angeles, and the New York Public Library.

To Al Cooley, for fancy footwork.

To those whose thoughts of music influenced mine: Peter Guralnick, Wynonie Harris, Delbert McClinton, Richard Meltzer, Jim Morrison, John Morthland, Joe Nick Patoski, Ezra Pound, and Billy Swan.

And to all who are due thanks but whom I've overlooked: tough.

Contents

COUNTRY

Thela in the New World

In the spring of 1607 a man named John Laydon, or Lydon, came to America. He was one of 100 men and 4 boys who left London in three ships a week before Christmas last. Like the others, he took with him clothes and grain and oil and axes and guns and knives. He also took a fiddle. It had come from Cremona before he was born, and it had belonged to his father. Carved into its dull, dark neck was a strange name: Thela.

All of the 104 perished, by "Swellings, Flixes, Burning Fevers, and by warres, and some departed suddenly, but for the most part they died of meere famine"; all but 38. With years, new ships came across the ocean and up the river to Jamestown, and in 1630, the year of John Laydon's fiftieth birthday, there were more than 2,500 souls.

First Laydon made soap ash, then pitch. In 1612, along with the others, he grew tobacco. In 1619 he got a girl from Liverpool, inexpensively. Her name was Lena. She was sixteen and soft, and loud when she drank. He liked her.

His life was as plain as burnished stone. He grew tobacco. He drank whiskey. He broke his leg in '37 and nearly died. He had six sons, and one of them drowned on a bright July morning. In the winter of 1645 he passed away in the night.

He fiddled "as a Man wilde by Fever," wrote his friend Nathaniel Powell. He loved the old tunes, the songs they played back home, and he made some "wondrous newe songs" that Powell mentioned by name in his diary. "Asked their Names, he reply'd the first Song is Devil's Bitche and the other is Drunk Negar, and then laught."

Two of Laydon's sons fiddled, and they had their own sons. It went on: Laydon's blood passed to the Carolinas and to Tennessee. The old fiddle passed too; repaired and dropped and rained upon and repaired and dropped.

Four men sit in a room without windows in Los Angeles. One is the president of the greatest record company in America. His skin is the color of fragile boredom, or mayonnaise. Another is a famous singer and songwriter who records for a subsidiary of the greatest record company in America. His name is not Laydon, or Lydon, but he has the blood, and he has the fiddle with the strange name carved into its neck. The other two men are his friends: his music publisher and his rhythm guitarist, who is also a singer and a songwriter.

The president has summoned the three so that they may hear an acetate of a song the president's young acquaintance has written. "It would be a natural for you," he says to the famous singer. "Just let me know what you think."

The acetate disk is placed on the turntable. In a moment it is obvious, to all but the president, that the song is a weak imitation of a hit the man not named Laydon had written in 1968. But they say nothing.

The tone-arm starts to skip and stutter upon the acetate. The rhythm guitarist takes a coin from his pocket and offers it to the president, to weigh the tone-arm with. The president regards the coin with feral hesitance. He takes it, examines it, and sticks it in his pocket.

"No," another says nicely. "Put it on the record."

The president gently places the coin on the black disk, near the label, where it goes around and around and around.

Orpheus, Gypsies, and Redneck Rock 'n' Roll

At the Henry E. Huntington Library and Art Gallery in San Marino, California, a young pedant, drudging out data for his doctoral thesis on the role of the industrial revolution in British broadside literature, hunches over the only surviving first edition of *The Tea-Table Miscellany*, a collection of balladry and popular verse compiled by Scots poet and wigmaker Allan Ramsay. Poring the frail, tawny pages of the fourth volume, printed in 1737, the pedant comes upon a ditty called "The Bottle Preferr'd":

> *As great as a monarch,*
> *The moments I pass,*
> *The bottle's my globe,*
> *And my scepter's the glass.*
> *The table's my throne,*
> *And the tavern's my court,*
> *The drawer's my subject,*
> *And drinking's my sport.*

At that same moment, at Big Ed's in Orlando, Florida, an unemployed poultry boner orders his seventh shot of Carstairs and slips a quarter into the jukebox. Doyle Holly's 1973 hit "Queen of the Silver Dollar" fills the barroom.

> *She's the queen of the Silver Dollar,*
> *And she rules this smoky kingdom.*

3

NICK TOSCHES

Her scepter is a wine glass,
And a bar stool is her throne. *

The pedant puts pencil to notebook, the drunken poultry boner burps and listens, and the continuum pulses on. Of course, Heraklitus was right. Everything flows; nothing abides.

An eighteenth-century lyric blaring from a jukebox in a topless bar is by no means the most bizarre example of what a crazy bastard sort of thing country music is. Its roots descend deeper into the past than those of any other popular music. In his *Diary* entry for January 2, 1666, Samuel Pepys wrote that a performance of the "little Scotch song of 'Barbary Allen' " by Mrs. Knepp, an actress, brought him "perfect pleasure." Writing in 1765, Oliver Goldsmith said that "an old dairy-maid sung me into tears with . . . 'The Cruelty of Barbary Allen.' " Centuries later, this same ancient ballad of mournful love is still being sung and recorded, and discovered anew by fresh ears.

In February of 1976, *Billboard* reported that Wink Martindale's 1959 recording of "Deck of Cards" had been added to the playlist of New York radio station WHN after several broadcasts of the record during the Christmas season had got a good response from WHN's audience. With a flourish of historicity, *Billboard* explained that "Deck of Cards" did not originate with Wink Martindale's 1959 hit on Dot Records, but that "T. Texas Tyler wrote 'Deck of Cards' about a young soldier being disciplined by his sergeant for having a deck of cards out in chapel. The song explains the deeper meaning the soldier sees in each card." Which is like mistaking an Egyptian potsherd for a piece of Pyrex.

T. Texas Tyler, born David Myrick about 1900 near Mena, Arkansas, had a Number Three country hit with "Deck of Cards" in the spring of 1948 on Four-Star, an independent Hollywood label. (Tyler had been performing "Deck of Cards" since 1939, when he had a radio show at WCHS in Charleston, West Virginia.) There have been assorted versions of Tyler's record by artists such as Rex Cross, Rusty

*"Queen of the Silver Dollar" by Shel Silverstein. Copyright © 1972 by Evil Eye Music, Inc. Used by permission.

4

Draper, Phil Harris, Nelson King, Wink Martindale, the Rainbow Four, Tex Ritter (whose cover was first, hitting the charts on July 10, 1948), Larry Robinson, Riley Shepard, the Stewart Family (who changed the recitation into a song), and Tex Williams. There have also been several parodies and derivatives. During the Korean War, Red River Dave, ever the opportunist, recorded a "Red Deck of Cards"; later Red Sovine cut "The Viet Nam Deck of Cards." Ferlin Husky did a "Hillbilly Deck of Cards," and Cowboy Copas did "Cowboy's Deck of Cards."

The truth of "Deck of Cards" is that an almost identical recitation was in use as a church sermon for at least a century before Tyler's birth. The sermon itself was little more than a British folk-tale variously called "The Perpetual Almanack," "The Gentleman Soldier's Prayer Book," "The Soldier's Bible," and "The Religious Card Player." Very likely "Deck of Cards" was a medieval standard. Tyler says he came across the recitation in his reading during 1938 and 1939. In 1954 he recorded a version of "Deck of Cards" for Blue Ribbon, a budget label that presented six ghost versions in each 78-rpm disk (Tyler, by then, was reduced to covering his own songs; the other artists in this same disk include an unknown Roy Clark singing "Run 'Em Off" and an unknown Jimmy Dean singing "Release Me"), and this version was titled "The Soldier's Prayer Book," probably the title under which Tyler first encountered it.

That such a scrap of kitsch has endured in a way that the writing of Roger Bacon has not says much about what's really timeless and what isn't; that the 1959 "Deck of Cards" was far more popular with pop audiences than with country audiences says much about who the real kitschmongers are.

At last glance, T. Texas Tyler was still around. After Four-Star he recorded for Decca, Capitol, and Starday. In the early sixties he became an ordained evangelist minister, and he and his wife, Claudia, traveled America doing God's P.R. And Wink Martindale, a former disk-jockey, hosts television game shows in L.A.

Well, I rocked over Italy and I rocked over Spain,
I rocked in Memphis, it was all the same,
Till I rocked into Africa and rolled off the ship
And seen them niggers doin' an odd-lookin' skip.
I parted the weeds and looked over the swamp,
And I seen them cats doin' the Ubangi Stomp.

So begins Warren Smith's 1956 rocker "Ubangi Stomp." The song was written by Charles Underwood, a producer, songwriter, and musician who was born in Iuka, Mississippi, on September 15, 1937. (In 1954 black alto saxophonist Earl Bostic had recorded an instrumental called "Ubangi Stomp" for King. Underwood's song bore no resemblance to Bostic's beyond the title.) Underwood was deeply involved in the seminal rock-and-roll scene at Sun Records in Memphis, and in 1959 he produced Charlie Rich's hit "Lonely Weekends" on the Phillips International label. In 1961 Charles and his wife moved to Los Angeles, and there in 1962 he engineered two hit records: "Monster Mash" by Bobby Pickett, and "The Lonely Bull" by Herb Alpert. In the spring of 1963 Underwood opened the Nashville West studio, which he operated until 1971. He recorded for Warner Brothers in 1966 as the Charlie Underwood Glide Band.

"Ubangi Stomp" typified the tough, churlish strain of country music that evolved in the 1950s. Known as rockabilly, it was the music of men such as Elvis Presley, Carl Perkins, and Jerry Lee Lewis. Aflash with images of sex, violence, and redneck existentialism, rockabilly was the glorious florescence of white rock-and-roll; it seemed such a sexy, pagan horror, such a dangerous new creature, that America feared it, preached against it, and tried to ban it. And yet, deep in its surly soul, rockabilly too carried ancientry. The juxtaposition of "Ubangi Stomp," part of the birth-scream of an era, and its flip-side, "Black Jack David," shard of another millenium, is an improbable but perfect symbol of modern country music's duality.

Warren Smith was born in Louise, a small town in western Mississippi, on February 7, 1932. He moved to Memphis in early 1953,

Warren Smith

several months after he left the Air Force. He was singing with Clyde Leoppard's Snearly Ranch Boys at the Cotton Club in West Memphis when Sam Phillips, owner of Sun Records and the first to record the rockabilly music of Elvis Presley and others, offered him an opportunity to cut some sides. In February 1956, Smith recorded "Rock 'n' Roll Ruby" for Sun, and it became a regional hit.

On March 30, 1956, Warren Smith went into the Sun studio at 706 Union Avenue in Memphis. With a band that consisted of a fiddler, a guitarist, a bassist, and a drummer, Smith cut four sides: "Who Took My Baby," "Movin' On," "I Couldn't Take the Chance," and "Black Jack David." Although none of the recordings from this session was released, at his next session, in August, Smith again cut "Black Jack David," along with "Ubangi Stomp," and the record was issued on September 1, 1956. "Black Jack David" was copyrighted in Smith's name several weeks later, on October 10.

Black Jack David come a-ridin' through the woods,
Singin' so loud and merry.
His voice kept ringin' through the green, green trees;
He spied a fair-haired maiden,
He spied a fair-haired maiden.

Would you forsake your husband dear?
Would you forsake your baby?
Would you forsake your fine, fine home
And go with Black Jack David,
Go with Black Jack David?

No, dear Jack, I cannot go
Away and leave my baby;
I cannot forsake my husband and home
And go with you, Black Jack David,
Go with you, Black Jack David.

Listen, dear lass, my name is Jack,
I've come from afar

Lookin' for a fair-haired lass like you;
Won't you come and be my bride,
Come and be my bride.

Yes, I'll forsake my husband dear,
And I'll forsake my baby,
I'll forsake my fine, fine home
And go with you, Black Jack David,
Go with you, Black Jack David.

Last night she slept on a fine feather bed
Beside her husband and baby,
Tonight she slept on the cold, cold ground
Beside old Black Jack David,
Beside old Black Jack David.

Smith left Sun Records in 1959, having scored one national pop hit, "So Long, I'm Gone." He went on to record for Liberty in Hollywood, on which label he had seven country hits during the years 1960 to 1964, Mercury in Nashville, Skill in Pasadena, Texas, then Jubal in Nashville. He now works as a safety man at Heat Control in Longview, Texas, where he has lived since the late 1960s with his wife and daughter.

In 1976, 20 years after he recorded it, I asked Warren Smith the source of the song "Black Jack David."

"I wrote it," he answered.

Cut to Athens, fourth century B.C. In his *Symposium*, Plato refers to an attempt made by Orpheus, mythical poet and son of Oegrus the harper and Muse Calliope, to rescue his wife from the land of the dead. This is the earliest known mention of Orpheus's wife, Eurydice, and of his adventure in the lower world. It's also the beginning of "Black Jack David."

In his fourth *Georgic*, completed in 29 B.C., the Roman poet Vergil wrote a full account of the myth of Orpheus and Eurydice. Aristaeus the shepherd, son of sea goddess Cyrene, had been playing about with Eurydice by the bank of a river. Pursuing her among the flora, Aristaeus saw Eurydice fall from the bite of a snake. She died. When Orpheus discovered this, he sank into pale despair. Eventually he pulled together the nerve to pass through the jaws of Taenarus into the underworld in search of his dead lady. He sang his petition so powerfully that Tartarus quaked. Proserpina, the death-bitch maxima, gave Orpheus permission to take his wife back to the plane of life, the conditional clause being that if he turned to look at Eurydice as he led her to the upper world, she would be returned to the land of snuff. In a moment of forgetfulness, Orpheus looked back. Pft.

Orpheus ambled and cried for seven months, and nothing could crack his sadness. One night during their sacred orgies in honor of Bacchus, the women of the Cicones, angered by Orpheus's refusal to fuck, tore his body apart. His meat was scattered about the countryside; his head was lobbed into the river Hebrus. Borne by the river's current, the head opened its bloodied mouth and called the name of Eurydice.

It was Ovid's retelling of the travails of Orpheus in his *Metamorphoses*, written in the first decade A.D., that brought the myth into later European culture, for by the twelfth century Ovid had become the most respected classical poet, and his influence spread throughout the Middle Ages. French, German, and Spanish renderings of *Metamorphoses* were in circulation before the end of the thirteenth century. Dante had Vergil guide him through the underworld, but it was Ovid whom he put in the highest place of honor allowable for a pagan poet. Ovid's version differed little from that of Vergil, except for some added drool-data, as when he informs in perfect hexameter that "Orpheus preferred to center his affections on boys of tender years, and to enjoy the brief spring and early flowering of their youth; he was the first to introduce this custom among the people of Thrace."

One of the most important popularizers of classical literature was the Roman Boethius, whose *De Consolatione Philosophiae*, written shortly before he had his head chopped off in 525, was one of the most widely read works in western Europe until the close of the Renaissance. Boethius too retold the legend of Orpheus and Eurydice, but interpreted it as a parable. "This fable," he wrote, "applies to all of you who seek to raise your minds to sovereign day. For whoever is conquered and turns his eyes to the pit of hell, looking into the inferno, loses all the excellence he has gained." Live and learn.

It was King Alfred's ninth-century translation of Boethius that ushered the Orpheus myth into medieval Britain. That the myth had entered the blood of British culture before the thirteenth century is attested to by such works as Welsh writer Walter Map's *De Nugis Curialium*. Completed about 1190, Map's book includes a passage, captioned *Item de fantasticis aparicionibus*, which tells of the death of a beloved wife, of her husband's grief, and of his success in finding her in the netherworld and bringing her back to the living. Classical myth becomes pop lore.

Here Ireland flows in. Celtic mythology contained a variety of legends in which supernatural men or women lured members of the opposite sex to come and dwell in the underworld. Ultimately, these legends derive from the ancient Celtic myth of the Rival Wooers, in which all the characters were gods and goddesses. *Leabhar na hUidhre*, an Irish manuscript written before 1106, tells one such tale, "Tochmarc Étaíne," or "The Wooing of Étaín." The story is this: Eochaid Airem, King of Ireland, weds beautiful young Étaín. Midir, the fairy ruler of the sidh, or underworld, of Brí Leith, had been Étaín's husband in a previous life, and he now approaches her to come live with him in the underworld. Étaín says that she will leave the king only if he gives her willingly to Midir. The fairy prince challenges the king to a series of chess games for high stakes, and loses them all. Unaware that Midir is hustling him, the king agrees to play one final game for whatever prize the winner wishes. Midir, of course, wins and demands the right to rub up against Étaín. The king stipulates a month's delay. Against the big day, he summons all the armies of Ireland to protect his palace from Midir's entry. Midir, being a fairy and all, appears mysteriously. The king keeps his bargain, and when Midir takes Étaín in his arms, the pair rise through the smoke-hole in the roof. The king and his men ravage all the fairy mounds in Ireland looking for Étaín. At the end of nine years' searching, the king is met with 60 women, all clones of Étaín, sent out by Midir. In time Étaín makes herself known, and the king brings her home in triumph. This tale, which probably made its first appearance in the ninth century, was still very much alive in the late Middle Ages.

Sometime in the twelfth century, an unknown bard of Brittany familiar with the classical myth, Walter Map's pop derivative of it, and the Irish legend of Étaín distilled the three strains into a melic poem called the *Lai d'Orphéy*. Although no manuscript of the lay has been discovered, it is referred to by name in several contemporary works.

Sir Orfeo is a thirteenth-century translation of the *Lai d'Orphéy*, which had probably been written in Old French or Anglo-Norman. The oldest of three *Sir Orfeo* manuscripts dates to the early fourteenth century. In a southwestern dialect of Middle English, the poem describes Lady Heurodis's abduction by a fairy king, Sir Orfeo's sadness and self-imposed exile, his discovery of the fairy palace after 10 years, and his recovery of Heurodis. Whoever adapted the lay into English showed a complete ignorance of its classical antecedents. He described Thrace as the ancient name for Winchester and ended his poem with this explanation of how it came into being:

> *Later, Breton harpers heard*
> *How this marvel had occurred,*
> *And made of it a pleasing lay,*
> *And gave to it the name of the king.*

So 'Orfeo' it is called today;
Fine is the lay, and sweet to sing.
Thus did Orfeo quit his care:
God grant that all of us so fare.

Over the centuries, *Sir Orfeo* devolved into a common ballad. This ballad seems not to have gained widespread popularity, for only two versions have been recorded. The first was transcribed from a performance by an elderly Scotsman in Unst, Shetland, in 1880 and published in February of that year in *The Leisure Hour.* The old man admitted that his memory had lost much of the original whole of the ballad, which he called "King Orfeo."

Der lived a king inta da aste,
 Scowan ürla grün;
Der lived a lady in da wast,
 Whar giorten han grün oarlac.

Dis king he has a huntin gaen,
He's left his Lady Isabel alane.

'Oh I wis ye'd never gaen away,
For at your hame is döl an wae.

'For da king o Ferrie we his daert,
Has pierced your lady to da hert.'

And aifter dem da king has gaen,
But whan he cam it was a grey stane.

The next and last time "King Orfeo" showed up was in April of 1947. Again it was found in Unst. In this later version there is little remaining but a shell.

Will ye come in into our ha',
Scowan Earl Grey,

13

Yes we'll come in into your ha',
For yetter kangra norla.

And we'll come in into your ha',
And we'll come in among ye a'.
First they played the notes o noy,
Then they played the notes o joy.

Then they played the good old gabber reel,
Scowan Earl Grey,
Which might a made a sick heart heal,
For gettar kangra norla.

Both these ballads reek death. They're skeletal, disjointed, and dull (who cares what "gettar kangra norla" means?). Mere archaeologic junk, like so many pieces of rotten hominid skull, these ballads are nothing but connections between the old and the new. "King Orfeo" is an evolutionary discard; it birthed a new brood of balladry, then fell. The abduction, the magick, the search were retained in the offspring of "King Orfeo," but the name of Orpheus was dropped for that of a new, but in his own way mythic, character. From *The Tea-Table Miscellany* of 1737, "Johny Faa, the Gypsie Laddie":

The gypsies came to our good lord's gate,
And wow but they sang sweetly;
They sang sae sweet, and sae very compleat,
That down came the fair lady.

And she came tripping down the stair,
And a' her maids before her;
As soon as they saw her well-far'd face,
They cooft the glamer o'er her.

Gae tak frae me this gay mantile,
And bring to me my plaidie,

14

COUNTRY

For if kith and kin and a' had sworn,
  I'll follow the gypsie laddie.

Yestreen I lay in a well-made bed,
  And my good lord beside me;
This night I'll ly in a tenant's barn,
  Whatever shall betide me.

Come to your bed, says Johny Faa,
  Oh come to your bed, my deary;
For I vow and I swear by the hilt of my sword,
  That your lord shall nae mair come near ye.

I'll go to bed to my Johny Faa,
  I'll go to bed to my deary;
For I vow and swear by what past yestreen,
  That my lord shall nae mair come near me.

I'll mak a hap to my Johny Faa,
  And I'll mak a hap to my deary,
And he's get a' the coat gaes round,
  And my lord shall nae mair come near me.

And when our lord came home at een,
  And speir'd for his fair lady,
The tane she cry'd, and the others reply'd,
  She's away with the gypsie laddie.

Gae saddle to me the black, black steed,
  Gae saddle and make him ready;
Before that I either eat or sleep,
  I'll gae seek my fair lady.

And we were fifteen well-made men,
  Altho' we were nae bonny;
And we were a' put down for ane,
  A fair young wanton lady.

Here, for a change, the sweet young thing doesn't particularly care to be rescued. No mistake about it: For all its similarities to *Sir Orfeo* and "King Orfeo," this ballad was driven by fresh winds.

Gypsies had arrived in Britain before the end of the fifteenth century, and soon began to make pests of themselves. Thievery and assault, along with fortune-telling scams, came to be synonymous with the word *gypsy.* In Scotland, where the gypsies made their British debut, Council Registers are full of charges brought against gypsies named Faa, Faw, or Fall (three spellings of the same name). This division of Faa gypsies seems already to have been established in southeast Scotland by 1470. In the Council Register of Aberdeen under the date of January 22, 1530, two female gypsies were arrested and described as servants of "George Faw, Earl of Egypt." At Falkland on February 15, 1540, James V signed a writ of the Privy Council of Scotland, which granted certain privileges to "John Faw, Lord and Earl of Little Egypt." On June 6, 1541, the writ was withdrawn and John Faw and his brood were ordered to leave Scotland within 30 days, under penalty of death. In 1554 Queen Mary gave "Johnne Faw" her royal pardon after he murdered someone. On July 10, 1616, "John Faw," his son James, and several other gypsies were sentenced to death. In 1624 six "Faas" and two other male gypsies were executed. By the nineteenth century, gypsies had forsaken the name Faa for others such as Allan, Barclay, Gordon, Kennedy, Shaw, Tait, and Young.

By the early part of the seventeenth century, one of these Faas, or all of them, had entered into popular legendry. The story has Orphic overtones. John VI, Earl of Cassillis, who was, according to *The Edinburgh Magazine and Literary Miscellany*, "commonly termed 'the grave and solemn Earl,' " wed Lady Jane Hamilton, daughter of Thomas, first Earl of Hadington. (In the year of Lady Jane's birth, 1607, Claudio Monteverdi created the first modern opera, *L'Orfeo*, based on the myth of Orpheus and Eurydice.) When Lord Cassillis was in England on business, the gypsy John Faw and several of his followers traveled to Cassillis and persuaded, some say by magick, the Lady to elope with him to England. She and Faw had not made it across the border when the Earl overtook them, murdering all the gypsies save one. Lady Jane was placed in a dungeon near Maybole, where she remained until her death in 1642.

It will never be known how much of the tale is truth. The *Woodrow MSS.* in the National Library of Scotland contain two letters in Lord Cassillis's hand, written after the death of his Lady Jane. In one, addressed to Robert Douglas, minister at Edinburgh, he wrote that "I finde it so harde to digest the want of a dear friend, such as my beloved yoke-fellow was." In the other, addressed to Lord Eglinton, he called his late wife a "dear bed-fellow." It is said Lord Cassillis wed again.

Legend has it that the lone survivor of Faw's band composed the ballad, but it is far more probable that the song was the work of one of the many professional ballad-makers who flourished in Britain from 1550 till the close of the nineteenth century. These men, most of whose names have long been lost, were the first of the breed later to be known as Tin Pan Alley hacks. They churned out songs and sold them for a shilling (rarely more) to printers, who published them in single folio sheets or in chapbooks of 8 to 16 pages, to be sold by peddlers who walked the streets or solicited door-to-door, sometimes singing the latest ballads as they moved along. Much of the work of ballad-makers (except for the period 1550 to 1580, when balladry was indulged in by literary men) was based on news.

Street balladry, the roots of traditional American music, was pop. The purest mountain airs, lustily pursued by sweaty, obsessive folklorists and concerned young things who believe there are people, *folk*, in the Blue Ridge Mountains who actually enjoy listening to Woody Guthrie records, were once the pop junk of urban Britain. In the preface to his 1888 anthology, *More Lyrics from the Song-Books of the Elizabethan Age*, A. H. Bullen denounced "the poor thin wretched stuff that one hears today." He might as well have been speaking about rock-and-roll. In a way, he was.

Street balladry didn't really die at the end of the nineteenth century. Its center became America, instead of Great Britain; its form of publication became phonograph records, instead of broadsides.

"The Gypsie Laddie" was a hit. Even Robert Burns used it in his 1808 *Reliquies*. When Charles Kirkpatrick Sharpe published a version of the ballad that he got "from the recitation of a peasant in Galloway" in the November 1817 issue of *The Edinburgh Magazine and Literary Miscellany*, he omitted several lines "on account of their indelicacy."

The ballad certainly arrived in America before 1750. It was popular in the New World, too. In almost every state the ballad flourished into the present century. (Versions have also been collected in Nova Scotia.) As it moved, "The Gypsie Laddie" changed. It became "Gyps of Davy," "The Gypsy Lover," "Gypsy Davy," "Black-Eyed Davy," "The Lady's Disgrace," "The Three Gypsy Laddies," and even "The Jewish Lady" in one Virginia version collected in 1932. Sex and violence became nursery rhyme in *The Magic Garden of My Book House*, a 1920 children's book by Olive Beaupré Miller that printed the ballad under the title "The Raggle, Taggle Gypsies."

One of the most popular American titles was "Black Jack David." The phrase "black jack" meant different things in different Scottish and English dialects: cockroach, black leather vest, caterpillar, dark sweetmeat made of treacle and spice; its significance in the ballad title is lost.

In October 1929 a duet with the glittery name of Professor and Mrs. I. G. Greer recorded "Black Jack Davy" for Paramount. Ten years later, in July 1939, Cliff Carlisle recorded "Black Jack David" for Decca. In October 1940 the Carter Family recorded it for Okeh. In 1945 T. Texas Tyler cut it for Four-Star. Carlisle says that he got his version from T. Texas Tyler, even though Tyler didn't record the song until several years after Carlisle's record; that Tyler copyrighted "Black Jack David" in August 1939, a month after Carlisle cut it, backs this up. The Carlisle record went like this:

> *Black Jack David come a-riding through the woods,*
> *Singing so loud and merry.*
> *His voice kept ringin' through the green, green trees,*
> *And he charmed the heart of a maiden,*
> *Charmed the heart of a maiden.*

And so on. Warren Smith was 7 years old when Carlisle's record came out. He was 13 when T. Texas Tyler's version was released.

"I wrote it."

You never heard it before that?

"Well, long, long time ago there was one called 'Black Jack David.' I guess I kinda got the idea from it, but I changed it around altogether. I remember hearin' this when I was quite young. One of those great big seventy-eight records. I heard it at some people's house. And I don't know how I ever came up with the idea that night for a second side of 'Ubangi Stomp.' I ran outa songs, and then all of a sudden I just got to hummin' it, and I set down then and started writin' it then, and we cut it the same night. I was kinda half-way crazy about it, y'know, but they kinda half-way banned it there in Memphis. I guess it was, uh, it was kinda like this man comin' through there while another man was gone from home and stole his wife, y'know?"

The Girl Singer

There is a motel in Cheyenne, at the junction of Interstates 80 and 25, called Holding's Little America. Cartoon penguins are everywhere: matchbooks, menus, cocktail napkins.

It is the end of July, and the week-long Frontier Days rodeo, held each year since 1896, is winding down. Tomorrow afternoon, Sunday, the winning ropers and wrestlers and riders will be given trophies, and it will be over until next year.

The girl singer and I are in a room, talking and drinking, among the penguins. It is four in the morning; the television is cold. The girl singer is dissipated. Earlier tonight she sang at Frontier Park. In the last 28 days she has sung at 27 other places, and taped a series of motorcycle safety commercials in Eugene. Next Thursday night, four towns from now, she will return to her home just north of Nashville. After six days of rest, she'll do it again, this time in the Southeast.

She is blowzy. The musculature of her face is still and sodden, and words come from the corners of her mouth thick and slow, like vomit from a man unconscious. She doesn't seem sad, just wasted. With the care of one who seems to be performing a ritual for the first time, she withdraws an envelope from a cosmetics case next to her on the bed. The envelope is opened, and several photographs and a small, thin piece of paper with writing on it are removed. After looking briefly, very briefly, at the piece of paper, she replaces it. She lays the photographs at the foot of the bed, away from her, so that they face me. There are five, black-and-white, each of a different age. The oldest print has a serrated border. A woman sits in a chair, her hair waved in the soft full curls of the 1940s, a small, pointed party hat tilted on her head. At her knee is a small boy, smiling, in a felt cowboy hat, spotted chaps, and miniature Western boots; he awkwardly holds a shiny cap pistol.

The second photograph shows a boy who appears to be in his early teens. He is of medium build, pale complexion. It seems to be winter, but it is difficult to tell. The boy is standing against a wooden wall, wearing a plaid cap and a hunting jacket. There is a rifle, a .22, propped against the wall behind him. He is smiling.

The third photograph shows the boy (by now it is obvious that the pictures are of the same person) in his late teens or early twenties. He is sitting, thinner than before, on a couch, and he has his arm around a pretty girl. He is making a funny face at the camera, a very dumb face really. He and the girl seem very familiar. Perhaps they are married, or brother and sister.

The fourth photograph shows the boy, or young man (he does not appear much older than in the third picture), standing in a softly dark suit with a group of other men, also wearing suits. One of these men is quite old. Everyone is smiling. There seems to be a mural in the background.

In the fifth photograph was a man I immediately recognized, a well-known country singer who was killed in a plane crash in the early 1960s. The young man, slightly older here but still youthful and soft and pale, is at his side in a restaurant, laughing over drinks and coffee and an ashtray full of cigarette butts like fat, white worms.

"Who is he?" asks the girl singer.

"Jim Reeves."

"No. The other one." She moved her hand across all five pictures.

"I don't know." Now it seemed funny, and a little annoying, like when you're a kid and an older cousin is playing a trick on you but you can't figure out why he's doing it; and it may not even be a trick so you don't want to laugh or yell "go away" either.

"Who does it remind you of?"

"No one," I say.

"When would you say this last picture is from?"

"About 1963, maybe '64. He looks the same as he did in all those pictures they published of him when he got killed."

"And the other guy doesn't remind you of anyone?"

I don't answer her this time, for she really is getting annoying.

Now she removes another photograph from the cosmetics case, one that hadn't been in the envelope. It is an early publicity photograph of herself. She looks quite different: Her hair is short and lacquered in the picture, and the airbrushing that was intended to make her face look like burnished ivory made it look instead like a soft, dull cheese. She places this photo with the others.

"They're all me," the girl singer says.

Loud Covenants

Words such as *realism, neoclassicism, minimalism,* and *Dada* are intellectual niceties, terms invented to describe esthetics. Each has a definition easily rote-learned; each has a clear, sensible origin. You can look at the word *Dada* and think, Yes, Tzara invented it, in 1916, to shock the world. It means "hobby-horse" in French. Cute.

But words such as *juke, jazz, honky-tonk,* and *rock-and-roll* are elusive. None of them was invented for the purposes of art; each seems to have its own pneuma, from which the art evolved, like dark, primeval word magick. Ancient black men say they quit playing blues because it's the devil's music. Pale white preachers yell against the sinfulness of rock-and-roll. And it is not impossible that the word *juke*, first encountered among the blacks of Florida and coastal Georgia, late in the last century, has the same source as the Wolof word *dzug*, which means to lead an evil, wicked life.

There is not a clue to the origin of the word *jazz.* Many of the black musicians who were active in New Orleans at the turn of the century were asked about the word, but none knew where it had come from. The November 15, 1890, issue of *The Mascot*, a weekly newspaper of New Orleans, described the music of a Basin Street jazz band as "a sad affliction." The band itself was described simply as "a nigger brass band." The earliest recorded use of the word is in "Uncle Josh in Society," a 1909 Columbia recording by Cal Stewart, whose series of rural-dialect monologues, described in a 1901 Columbia catalogue as "Uncle Josh Weathersby's Laughing Stories," began in 1898 and remained popular till the late 1920s. The line is, "One lady asked me if I danced the jazz." In the June 17, 1917, issue of *The Times-Picayune*, a writer, in his finest remedial English, asked, "Why is the jass music, and, therefore, the jass band?" He damned the music as "indecent" and a "vice," and concluded that "its possibilities of harm are great." The title of a jazz song, popular among Storyville performers of the day, responded indirectly to *The Times-Picayune*: "Kiss My Fuckin' Ass."

The phrase *honky-tonk* was first encountered in the east Texas–Louisiana–Oklahoma area. In the February 24, 1894, issue of *The Daily Ardmoreite*, published in Ardmore, Oklahoma, is the report that "the honk-a-tonk last night was well attended by ball-heads, bachelors and leading citizens." (Wait, let me check that. Yes, it's right here: "ball-heads.") New Orleans bars were sometimes referred to as tonks by blacks of the period. The first appearance of the phrase in a song is in "Everything Is Hunky Dory down in Honky Tonk Town," from the Tin Pan Alley musical *Everything*, staged at the New York Hippodrome in 1918 with a cast that included Houdini. In 1924 Fletcher Henderson and His Club Alabam Orchestra recorded " 'Those Broken Busted' Can't Be Trusted Blues (A Honky-Tonk Blues)" for Vocalion. The next year, Bennie Moten's Kansas City Orchestra cut "Sister Honky-Tonk" for Okeh. Meade Lux Lewis helped birth boogie-woogie in 1927 with his Paramount record "Honky Tonk Train Blues."

In country music, honky-tonk came to be associated with the loud, small-group sound that developed in the redneck bars of east Texas oil-boom towns: amplified guitars and lyrics of sex and whiskey. It's odd that Al Dexter, an east Texan born in 1902, who wrote and recorded "Pistol Packin' Mama," one of the classic honky-tonk songs (and the first country song to make *Your Hit Parade*, which censored "beer" from the song's lyrics), doesn't recall hearing the phrase until 1937. In those days, Dexter wrote songs with a guy named James B. Paris.

"One day I went to see Paris, and he said, 'I thought of a title last night that'll set the woods on fire.' I asked him what it was, and he said 'Honky Tonk Blues.' I asked him where he got that idea. I never heard the word, so I said, 'What is a honky-tonk?' So he said, 'These beer joints up and down the road where the girls jump in cars and so on.'

I said, 'I never thought about it like that.' He said, 'Use your thinker-upper and let's write a song like that.' "

Dexter and Paris copyrighted their song on February 26, 1937. There had been songs with similar titles ("Hunkie Tunkie Blues" by Hunkie Smith in 1930, "Honky Tonk Blues" by Pat Shelton in 1936), but they weren't country songs. "Honky Tonk Blues" led to Dexter's recording contract with Vocalion and a storm of honky-tonk fever in country music. By 1938 even Roy Acuff was singing about "Honky Tonk Mamas." Dexter's late awareness of the phrase is especially weird in light of the fact that he operated an east Texas honky-tonk, the Round-Up Club, in the early thirties. Was this club patronized by ball-heads? History is silent.

In 1893, before any of these words appeared in print, anthropologist Richard Wallaschek wrote in his book *Primitive Music* that "the most striking feature of all the savage songs is the frequent occurrence of words with no meaning whatever." A-womp-bop-a-lu-bop, a-womp-bam-boom.

Rock-and-roll. Both verbs came to the English tongue during the Middle Ages, and were soon used as skin-thrill metaphors. "My throbbing heart shall rock thee day and night," wrote Shakespeare in *Venus and Adonis.* An early nineteenth-century sea chanty included the line, "Oh do, me Johnny Bowker, come rock 'n' roll me over." A lyric found in the ceremonial Fire Dance of Florida's obeah worshippers was, "Bimini gal is a rocker and a roller."

In the fall of 1922, blues singer Trixie Smith cut a song called "My Daddy Rocks Me (With One Steady Roll)" for Black Swan Records. It was a hit. The Southern Quartet, a black group that recorded for Columbia, did a version of the song in 1924, under the title "My Man Rocks Me (With One Steady Roll)." By the next year, white kids were on to the song; in February 1925 Harold Ortli and His Ohio State Collegians recorded the song under its original title for Okeh. In 1929 Jimmie Noone and Tampa Red both had versions released by Vocalion.

Trixie Smith's record inspired many lyrical elaborations: "Rock That Thing" by Lil Johnson (Vocalion, 1929), "Rock Me Mama" by Ikey

Robinson (Brunswick, 1929), "Rocking and Rolling" by Bob Robinson (Champion, 1930, but unissued), "I'm a Steady Rollin' Man" by Robert Johnson (Vocalion, 1937), "Rock Me Daddy" by Georgia White (Decca, 1937), "Rock It for Me" by Mildred Bailey (Vocalion, 1938), and others.

The metaphor also has a spiritual life, as shown by black gospel recordings such as "Rock, Church, Rock" by Clara Smith (Columbia, 1926) and "Rock My Soul" by Mitchell's Christian Singers (Vocalion, 1939). "She was found with child of the Holy Ghost," says the Bible, and He's still rocking and rolling them in the South. In *White Spirituals in the Southern Uplands*, George Pullen Jackson described an interracial convention of Holy Rollers he attended in Cleveland, Tennessee, in September 1929.

"The spirit moved some to dance, others to speak in the unknown tongue, to shout, to jerk, or to fall in a dead trance. Mourners in ever-increasing numbers fell on their knees, elbows in a folding chair, at the altar, while the exhorters clapped hands to the time of the music, urged the kneeling ones to 'come through,' I imagined, and were quite beside themselves at the appearance of even a faint smile on the face of the praying sinner.

"After half an hour of this, the singing came to an end. Also the instrument strummers, worn out, dropped out one by one, leaving only the piano player and a tambourine whacker, whom I could not see, to carry on the steady and almost terrifying rhythmic noise. Terrifying because it impressed me as being the production of the wild, subconscious human animal, one which we seldom come upon in such frightfully self-regimented herds. But the extreme mesmeric orgies of such primitive groups have been often enough described. And after all, my purpose is simply to make clear how the indigenous song merges into the hypnotic rhythmizing used in this indigenous type of religious practice."

Holy Roller cults are still alive in the South and in some Northern black urban areas. There is still shock in their worship. "And they shall take up serpents, and if they drink any deadly thing, it shall not hurt them," says the Bible, so some sects dance with rattlesnakes about their necks and drink "salvation cocktails," made of strychnine and water.

The eighth line of Psalm 22 is "He trusted in the Lord." But the Hebrew word translated as "trusted" is transliterated *gahlahl* which didn't mean trust. The 1560 Geneva Bible gave a literal translation of the line: "He roled in the Lord."

The schizophrenia of the rock-and-roll metaphor was the inspiration for "Holy Roll," a funny, dirty 1931 Columbia record by Rufus and Ben Quillian.

By the early thirties, rock-and-roll was more than a fuck-phrase. It described an elusive style of music, a new sensuality of rhythm. In 1931 Duke Ellington recorded "Rockin' in Rhythm" for Victor, and in 1934 Red Nichols cut the same piece for white folks.

In *Transatlantic Merry-Go-Round*, a film released by United Artists in the fall of 1934, the Boswell Sisters (Martha, Connie, and Helvetia, all from New Orleans) sang a song called "Rock and Roll." It was written by Sidney Clare and Richard A. Whiting, a pair of Tin Pan Alley authors born in the 1890s. The Boswell Sisters recorded the song with Jimmy Crier and His Orchestra on October 4 in Los Angeles, and it was issued by Brunswick to coincide with the movie. On October 23, Joe Hayne and His Orchestra covered the song for Melotone. Gladys Presley of Tupelo was pregnant that "Rock and Roll" autumn.

The elusive rhythm spread, became more defined: "Rocking the Blues" by the Port of Harlem Jazzmen, featuring Albert Ammons on piano (Brunswick, 1939), "Keep Rockin' " by Harlan Leonard and His Rockets (Bluebird, 1940), "Rocking the Boogie" by Cecil Gant (Four-Star, 1946), "Good Rockin' Tonight" by Roy Brown (DeLuxe, 1947), "Rockin' the Blues" by Pee Wee Crayton (Modern, 1947), "Shout and Rock" by Billy Williams (Atlantic, 1948), "Rock and Roll" by the Flairs (Modern, 1949), "Rock & Roll" by Wild Bill Moore (Modern, 1949), "Rock the Joint" by Jimmy Preston (Gotham, 1949), "Rockin' " by the Robins (Modern, 1949), "We're Gonna Rock" by Cecil Gant doing business as Gunter Lee Carr (Decca, 1950), "Rock It" by Jimmy McCracklin (Modern, 1950), "Rock 'n' Roll" by John Lee Hooker (Modern, 1950), "Rockin' and Rollin' " by Lil Son Jackson (Imperial, 1950), "Rockin' Blues" by the Johnny Otis Congregation

(Savoy, 1950), "Rockin' with Red" by Piano Red (RCA-Victor, 1950), "Rocking After Midnight" by Lowell Fulson (Swing Time, 1950), "All I Do Is Rock" by the Robins (Crown, 1951), "Let's Rock Awhile" by Amos Milburn (Aladdin, 1951), "Rock Little Baby" by Cecil Gant (Decca, 1951), "Rock Me All Night Long" by the Ravens (Mercury, 1952), and "Rock, Rock, Rock" by Willis Jackson (Atlantic, 1952) and Amos Milburn (Aladdin, 1953).

Almost all these records were by blacks, and all of them were popular among blacks. Some were primitive but pure rock-and-roll. Roy Brown's 1947 "Good Rockin' Tonight" was a jump blues, the most popular sort of music among urban blacks of the 1940s (and very popular among whites, as record-sales patterns and TV appearances by such jump blues artists as Louis Jordan indicate). In the summer of 1948, Wynonie Harris cut a version of the same song for King, and the new version was a hit. Harris's "Good Rockin' Tonight" was a jump blues also, but it was wilder, less mellow than the usual jump blues record. It rocked.

It is impossible to discern the first modern rock record, just as it is impossible to discern where blue becomes indigo in the spectrum. It is right to say, however, that by 1950 black music was rocking strong. Imperial issued Fats Domino's first record, "The Fat Man," in 1949, and it sold well. In 1951 occurred several pure and unmistakable rock-and-roll hits: "Sixty Minute Man" by the Dominoes on Federal, "It Ain't the Meat" by the Swallows on King, "Rocket '88'" and its sequel "My Real Gone Rocket" by Jackie Brenston and His Delta Cats on Chess.

The Dominoes' "Sixty Minute Man" was not only the biggest rhythm-and-blues (R&B) hit of 1951, but also the first rock-and-roll record to make the pop charts, which is especially surprising in light of its theme. Billy Ward, ringleader of the Dominoes, was born in Los Angeles on September 19, 1921, and began composing classical pieces when he was a teenager. He was a Golden Gloves champion, soldier, journalist, and voice coach at Carnegie Hall before forming the Dominoes in the late forties. In 1950 he enlisted 17-year-old Clyde McPhatter as lead tenor singer, and by the end of 1951 the Dominoes were

One of the first pure rock records. Sam Phillips produced it in Memphis in March 1951. Singer Jackie Brenston's name was used on the label, but the band was really Ike Turner's, an 18-year-old piano-player and disk-jockey from Clarksdale, Mississippi.

the most famous black group in America. In 1955 they cut a salty epilogue to their biggest hit: "Can't Do Sixty No More."

After "Sixty Minute Man," other black rock-and-roll records appeared in the pop charts: "Crying in the Chapel" by the Orioles (Jubilee, 1953), "Gee" by the Crows (Rama, 1954), "Sh-Boom" by the Chords (Cat, 1954), "Hearts of Stone" by the Charms (DeLuxe, 1954), and "Ling, Ting, Tong" by the Five Keys (Capitol, 1954) and the Charms (DeLuxe, 1955). But none of these, except for "Sixty Minute Man," was a hard-ass rock-and-roll record, and the collective sound was closer to that of the Ink Spots than to that of Wynonie Harris and the others.

There were many hard-rocking country records in the years before Elvis Presley's debut. Although it was never as popular among whites as it was among blacks, the metaphor had been used by early country singers. Uncle Dave Macon was the first to use it, when he cut "Rock About My Saro Jane" for Vocalion in 1927. He later said he got the song in 1887, from black singers in Nashville. Jimmie Davis recorded "Rockin' Blues" for Victor in 1932, but it was not released. Cliff Carlisle cut "My Rockin' Mama" for Bluebird in 1936. Buddy Jones recorded "Rockin' Rollin' Mama" for Decca in 1939.

As black music began rocking in the forties, a parallel development occurred in country music. It was called hillbilly boogie, and it was pioneered by men such as the Delmore Brothers, Moon Mullican, and Arthur Smith. The first country boogie record was "Boogie Woogie," recorded in 1939 for Bluebird by an obscure Southerner named Johnny Barfield, who accompanied himself on guitar. In some of their King releases, such as "Freight Train Boogie" (1946) and "Whatcha Gonna Gimme" (1952), the Delmore Brothers went beyond boogie into an effervescent sort of country rock. Pianist Freddie Slack and sexy Texas singer Ella Mae Morse cut "House of Blue Lights" for Capitol in 1946, and it was such a fine, tough rocker that Chuck Berry recorded it twelve years later. Red Foley's "Tennessee Saturday Night" on Decca was one of the best-selling country records of 1948, and it rocked. "Rootie Tootie," Hank Williams's third MGM release, cut in 1947, was a jivey rocker, whirling with nonsense lyrics, funky call-and-response, and hot licks. Carl Perkins recalls that the rhythm of Hank's 1953 "Kaw-Liga" inspired Sun thinking. (And there is persistent rumor that Hank Williams left behind a tape of R&B performances, but that it's been suppressed in the interests of his image.) A handful of Tennessee Ernie Ford's early records, on Capitol, such as "Smokey Mountain Boogie" (1949), "Shotgun Boogie" (1950), and "I Don't Know" (1953), are among the best and strongest examples of country music's gropings toward rock-and-roll. The Maddox Brothers and Rose, a West Coast Okie group, recorded stuff that not only rocked, but also contained many of the vocal fireworks—yelps, screams, howls —that became watermarks of rockabilly. They cut "New Mule Skinner Blues" (a version of Jimmie Rodgers's "Blue Yodel No. 8") for Four-Star in the late forties; it was copied by the Fendermen in 1960, and became a Number Five rock hit. Their "Hangover Blues" (Decca, 1952) is pure gutter-rock. In 1956, the year Elvis broke, the Maddox Brothers and Rose recorded "The Death of Rock & Roll" for Columbia.

In 1949 Atlantic released "Blues Rock" by Texas Johnny Brown and His Blues Rockers. The Atlantic files indicate that it was a country record, but apparently no copies of it have been found. This may be the first instance of a country performer styling himself as a rocker. In early 1954, a few months before Elvis cut his first sides, Joe Almond and His Hillbilly Rockers recorded "Gonna Roll and Rock" for Trumpet Records of Jackson, Mississippi.

The first white rock-and-roll star was Bill Haley. He was born William John Clifton Haley in the Detroit suburb of Highland Park, in March 1927. When he was seven, his family moved to Booth Corner, a small town in southeastern Pennsylvania. During his high-school years, Haley began playing country music. As a disk-jockey at WSNJ in Bridgeport, New Jersey, in 1945, Haley took the name Yodeling Bill Haley. One of his idols was Bob Wills, and when Haley cut his first records, for the Cowboy label in 1950, he called his group Bill Haley & the Four Aces of Western Swing. The Cowboy records included versions of recent country hits: George Morgan's "Candy Kisses," Red Foley's "Tennessee Border," and Hank Williams's "Too Many Parties, Too Many Pals."

After Cowboy, Haley cut several records for Center, Keystone, and Atlantic. Late in 1951 he cut his first rock records, for Holiday, a Philadelphia label run by Dave Miller. His Holiday debut was a version of Jackie Brenston's "Rocket '88'," which had been a Number One R&B hit earlier in the year. Haley continued to look to the R&B charts for inspiration. In 1952 he cut a pair of duets with someone named

Bill Haley and His Comets. Billy Williamson (second from left) played steel guitar. Rudy Pompelli (third from left) played saxophone.

Loretta ("Bill and Loretta with the Saddlemen," the labels read): "Pretty Baby," a Griffin Brothers R&B hit of the year before, and "I'm Crying," which Memphis Slim had cut earlier in 1952.

Haley still showed his ties to country music. His last record for Holiday was "Jukebox Cannonball," a thin parody of "Wabash Cannonball," and when he began recording for Essex (also a Dave Miller label), his first release was "Icy Heart" in 1952, plainly inspired by Hank Williams's "Cold, Cold Heart" of 1951.

The flip-side of "Icy Heart," however, was "Rock the Joint," a wholly violent and fiery rocker—not merely a cover of an R&B hit (Jimmy Preston's 1949 original was on Gotham, a Philadelphia independent), but a lumination.

1951—Japanese Peace Treaty signed.
1952—White boy rocks.
1953—First atomic-powered submarine launched.

In the spring of 1953 came Haley's first hit, "Crazy, Man, Crazy." It rose to the Top Twenty, at a time when "Song from Moulin Rouge" by Percy Faith was Number One. "Crazy, Man, Crazy" was the first white rock hit, but already, somewhere between "Rock the Joint" and the spring of 1953, Haley had let the fire die. In "Rock the Joint" he reveled, in "Crazy, Man, Crazy" he merely performed.

Decca signed Haley in 1954, largely on the basis of "Crazy, Man, Crazy." In April of that year, Haley recorded "(We're Gonna) Rock Around the Clock," which went unnoticed. His second Decca release, a cover of Joe Turner's "Shake, Rattle and Roll," hit the Top Ten. His next record, "Dim, Dim the Lights," crossed over to the R&B charts.

"Rock Around the Clock" was written by a pair of Tin Pan Alley veterans, lyricist Max Freedman and composer Jimmy DeKnight. Freedman, born in 1895, had written "Sioux City Sue," "Song of India," and "Blue Danube Waltz." DeKnight was really James Myers of Myers Music. When Evan Hunter's 1954 novel, *Blackboard Jungle*, was made into a movie, James Myers was chosen as technical advisor (perhaps because he was known to have several acquaintances under the age of 65—Max Freedman, for instance). Myers suggested that "Rock Around the Clock" be used as the film's theme song.

Blackboard Jungle was released in March, 1955. Bosley Crowther of *The New York Times* questioned whether the film was "a desirable stimulant to spread before the young." *Blackboard Jungle* was banned in Memphis. Clare Booth Luce, ambassador to France, demanded the film be withdrawn as an entry at the Venice Film Festival, and so it was. What fine publicity.

In May "Rock Around the Clock" hit the charts, and it rose to Number One. In June it crossed over to the R&B charts, where it hit Number Four.

"Rock Around the Clock" became the best-selling rock record in history, with sales of almost 17 million to date. But what I find more fascinating, more important about the record, and about Bill Haley, is this: "Rock Around the Clock" was recorded three months before Elvis made his first record, and it was a hit nine months before Elvis appeared on the pop charts. Viewing Haley's earlier records, such as "Rock the Joint," as the first white rock-and-roll, and "Rock Around the Clock" as not only the first Number One rock hit, but also the first clear example of rock gone wholly astray, of fake Tin Pan Alley rock, one can plainly see that in the brief span from 1952 to 1955 rock-and-roll had already risen and fallen. When Elvis broke in early 1956, it had all gone down already. All that remained was for it to be done again, grander and louder; end cycle. The year the Beatles broke, 1963, Elvis was reduced to "Bossa Nova Baby," and Bill Haley, even further into the dim, was doing stuff like "Midnight in Washington" for Newtown Records. And in 1976 my buddy Richard Meltzer saw two 14-year-old girls looking through the bins in a Los Angeles record store. One came upon a Beatles album and called to her friend, "Hey, look! Paul McCartney was in a band before Wings."

In 1952, the year of "Rock the Joint," 29-year-old disk-jockey Alan Freed was hosting his *Moondog Rock and Roll Party*, a nightly show broadcast from WJW in Cleveland. Freed's programming of black music for white kids was actually the idea of Leo Mintz, an acquaintance of Freed who operated the biggest record store in Cleveland. In March 1952, Freed promoted his first concert, which he called a Moondog Ball, at the Cleveland Arena. The Arena had a capacity of 10,000, and there were about 9,000 tickets sold in advance. On the night of the show, between 20,000 and 30,000 kids showed up. They smashed the doors open, overwhelmed the police, and screamed. "Everybody had such a grand time breaking into the Arena," said Freed, "that they didn't ask for their money back."

On September 8, 1954, Freed broadcast his first program at WINS in New York City. In New York Freed called the show simply *Rock and Roll Party* after he was enjoined from including the word *Moondog* by a large blind person named Moondog, who was a familiar figure in the midtown area. In 1953 Moondog had cut some jazz percussion sides for Decca. (He continues to be seen alurk in Manhattan streets, with his staff, horned Viking helmet, flowing robe, and long white whiskers. In the late sixties he cut an album for Columbia.)

Freed became the king of rock-and-roll, and the shows he produced at the Brooklyn Paramount are legendary. At his 1956 Labor Day week shows, he grossed $221,000, an unheard-of take for a rock promoter in those days.

A scandal bloomed near television quiz shows in 1959. On November 4 of that year, 12-year-old Patty Duke, who was then working on Broadway in *The Miracle Worker*, revealed before Congressman Owen Harris's Subcommittee on Legislative Oversight that she had been given the answers in advance of her appearance on *The $64,000 Challenge* in 1958. Duke had won $32,000 as an expert on singing groups. The person who gave her the answers was Shirley Bernstein, associate producer of the program and sister of culture snoid Leonard Bernstein. *The New York Post*'s headline covered the entire front page: "THEY EVEN FIXED THE KID." There was a photo of small, smiling Patty.

The TV payola scandal spread to radio. Disk-jockeys were accused of taking money in return for airplay. Buy some spins; buy some hits. On occasion the currency was not cash, but small parcels of white stuff, or the ministrations of vagina and jowl.

New York district attorney Frank S. Hogan, who was among the first of the inquisitors of TV payola in the summer of 1958, obtained commercial-bribery indictments against eight fast-talking humans. One was convicted, and two pleaded guilty and paid fines; charges against the other five were dropped. Alan Freed was one of the two who pleaded guilty. In 1960 he was indicted on the charge of accepting $30,650 from six record companies in exchange for, ahem, promotional services. Freed was indignant: "This is the backbone of American business." He changed his plea to guilty in the end, and in return was handed a six-month suspended sentence and a $300 fine. Later he was indicted on charges of evading payment of taxes on $37,920 in payola. The king withdrew to an exile in Palm Springs, where he died of uremia in 1965.

Monday, July 5, 1954. The most popular albums in America are Jackie Gleason's *Tawny,* Frank Sinatra's *Songs for Young Lovers*, and the soundtrack of *The Glenn Miller Story*. The top song in the Hit Parade is "Three Coins in the Fountain." The biggest-selling R&B artists are the Midnighters, and the biggest-selling country artist is Webb Pierce. There has been a white rock-and-roll star: Bill Haley.

On this summer day, something is happening in Memphis that will overwhelm the whole of American music. Within the Sun Record Company at 706 Union Avenue, Sam Phillips is cutting a first session on a local punk named Elvis Presley.

Sam Phillips had got into the record business by way of radio. Born in Florence, Alabama, in 1925, Phillips began working as a radio announcer after dropping out of high school in 1941. At night, he studied engineering, podiatry, and embalming. In 1942 he was a disk-jockey at WLAY in Muscle Shoals, and the next year at WHSL in Decatur. In 1945 he worked at WLAC in Nashville, and from 1946 to 1949 he worked at WREC in Memphis, where he also promoted shows at the Hotel Peabody.

With the money he had saved as a disk-jockey and promoter, Phillips opened a recording studio in 1950 at 706 Union Avenue, where he made recordings of Southern blacks and leased them to independent labels: Chess, Modern, Meteor, Trumpet, and others. He also recorded weddings and the drolleries of Rotarians, transcribed them onto one-sided LPs, and charged nine dollars a throw.

One of the early records that Phillips cut and leased was Jackie Brenston's "Rocket '88'," recorded in March 1951. Some of the record's success as a rocker must be attributed to Phillips. He added extra amplification to Willie Kizart's guitar work, and in doing so added much brash dimension to the overall bad-ass sound of the record.

Other bluesmen whom Sam Phillips recorded were Bobby Bland, Little Milton, James Cotton, Sleepy John Estes, Earl Hooker, Walter Horton, Howlin' Wolf, B. B. King, and Joe Hill Louis.

In 1952 Sam decided to start his own record label. He took his brother Judd on as partner and paid a commercial artist on Beale Street to design a logo for the label, which Sam called Sun.

The early months of Sun Records are a faded picture. The first known Sun record, "Blues in My Condition" coupled with (C / W) "Selling

A 1951 check signed to Chester Burnett (Howlin' Wolf) by Sam C. Phillips. Wolf was produced by Phillips from late 1950 to the summer of 1952.

My Whiskey," by Jackie Boy and Little Walter, is Sun 174. Phillips cut these sides by Jack Kelly and Walter Horton in the Union Avenue studio on February 25, 1952, and assigned the coupling the catalogue number 174. (Independent labels rarely inaugurated with logical designations. Instead of giving their first releases catalogue numbers such as 1 or 100 or 1000, they chose numbers with personal meanings—lucky numbers. For instance, 174 may have signified a girlfriend's address or a policy number Phillips had hit with. Later on, independent labels took to giving their first releases high numbers, to fool distributors into thinking the label had been in business for a long time, and thus received better treatment or credit.) It is not known, however, when this first Sun record was issued, if indeed it was.

In any case, Sun started as a blues label. Walter Horton, Joe Hill Louis, Rufus Thomas, Memphis Ma Rainey, the Prisonaires, and Junior Parker were among the first Sun artists.

Sun's first country record was "Silver Bells" by the Ripley Cotton Choppers, a quartet from Ripley, Tennessee. It was released in October 1953, with HILLBILLY stamped in red upon its yellow label. With subsequent releases, it became obvious that Phillips was trying to wrest a new sound from his country sessions.

"Boogie Blues" by Earl Peterson, a country singer from Lansing, Michigan, who had known Phillips since his disk-jockey days, was issued in March 1954. This wry, uptempo song featured a yodeling vocal. It also bore the HILLBILLY stamp. Peterson was basically an old-line country singer, but "Boogie Blues" possessed a lively, youthful edge. The next year, Peterson recorded the song for Columbia.

Hardrock Gunter's "Gonna Dance All Night" was released in May of 1954. Sidney Louie Gunter, born in Birmingham, Alabama, on September 18, 1918, had been a disk-jockey since 1939 and a recording artist since the late forties. He was best known for his 1948 "Birmingham Bounce" on the Bama label. Red Foley and Leon McAuliffe both covered "Birmingham Bounce" in 1950; Foley's version, on Decca, was a Number One country hit. In 1951 R&B singer Amos Milburn covered the song for Aladdin. That same year, Hardrock became 1st Lieutenant Sid Gunter and was stationed in Fort Jackson, South Carolina. Before coming to Sun, he recorded for Bullet, Decca, and MGM. He continued to record for small labels (Cullman, Cross Country, Emperor) into the sixties, when he worked as a disk-jockey at WWVA in Wheeling, West Virginia, before retiring to Golden, Colorado. (He had been a member of the WWVA Jamboree when he recorded for Sun.) In 1963 he cut an atrocity for Starday called "Hillbilly Twist."

"Gonna Dance All Night" and its flip, "Fallen Angel," were a new sort of country record, inspired perhaps by Bill Haley's Essex sides. "We're gonna rock 'n' roll," sang Gunter, and Sam Phillips smiled.

A record cut the same day as "Gonna Dance All Night," and released in June 1954, came closer to the panting It: "My Kind of Carryin' On" by Doug Poindexter and the Starlite Wranglers. It fluttered, shook like a creature flirting with madness. Sam must have slept well that night.

"My Kind of Carryin' On" was Poindexter's only Sun single. In 1955 he retired from the music business after the break-up of his band. His lead guitarist, Scotty Moore, and his bass-player, Bill Black, had joined with a new singer. Today Poindexter sells insurance in Memphis.

Monday, July 5, 1954. Rock-and-roll exists. Sam Phillips, Elvis Presley, Scotty Moore, and Bill Black are in Sun's poky, 30-by-20-foot studio messing with "Blue Moon of Kentucky," a song Bill Monroe and His Blue Grass Boys had cut for Columbia in 1945. Phillips has that weird bastard sound in the dampness of his brain, and he looks at Presley and hopes.

Finally the sound is in the air—materialized, magic—captured on magnetic tape. It's a curious, physical sound. Rockabilly they would come to call it in a year's time.

Sam Phillips grins. "Hell, that's different," he says. "That's a pop song now, Little Vi. That's *good.*"

Elvis Aron Presley was 19 then (he was born in Tupelo, Mississippi, on January 8, 1935). Six years earlier, in 1948, his family had moved to Memphis, and in the spring of 1953 Elvis was graduated from Humes High School. His picture in *The Herald,* the Humes High yearbook, shows a boy with sideburns, Corinthian pompadour, and a hint of acne. He had participated, the yearbook says, in R.O.T.C., Biology Club, English Club, History Club, and Speech Club. The summer after graduation, Presley went to work for the Precision Tool Company. He left that job after a brief time and began working at the Crown Electric Company, which paid him $42 a week to drive a truck.

On a Saturday afternoon in 1953 (Haley's "Crazy, Man, Crazy" was in the air), Elvis made his first visit to the Sun studio. As a side-line operation, Phillips still maintained his Memphis Recording Service, administered by Marion Keisker, former Miss Radio of Memphis. It was to the Memphis Recording Service, not Sun Records, that Elvis came that afternoon. He paid Keisker the four-dollar charge, entered the studio with his acoustic guitar, and recorded two songs directly onto a double-sided 10-inch acetate disk. On one side Elvis cut "My Happiness," which the Ink Spots had had a hit with on Decca in 1948. On the other side he did "That's When Your Heartaches Begin," a mawkish ballad written by Zeb Turner and recorded by Bob Lamb on Dot in 1951.

Struck by Presley's voice, Marion Keisker recorded the end of "My Happiness" and the whole of "That's When Your Heartaches Begin" on a length of discarded tape. Seventeen years later, Marion Keisker MacInnes told Elvis biographer Jerry Hopkins, "The reason I taped Elvis was this: Over and over I remember Sam saying, 'If I could only find a white man who had the Negro feel, I could make a billion dollars.' This is what I heard in Elvis, this . . . what I guess they now call 'soul,' this Negro sound. So I taped it. I wanted Sam to know."

Keisker made a note of Presley's address, 464 Alabama Street, and the next time she saw Phillips she played the tape of Elvis's performance. Sam seemed mildly interested, but did not pursue the matter.

On January 4, 1954, Elvis returned to the Memphis Recording Service. Marion Keisker was not in, but Phillips was. They spoke, Sam calmly and plainly and easily, Elvis nervously. He paid Sam four dollars and cut another acetate: "I'll Never Stand in Your Way," a 1941 country song written by Clint Horner, and "Casual Love Affair."

In the early summer of 1954, about eight months after Elvis had first visited the Sun studio, Sam Phillips received a demonstration record of a song called "Without You," cut in Nashville by an unknown black singer. Sam was so impressed by the demo that he wanted to release it on Sun. He called Nashville in search of the singer and to obtain permission to issue the record. He was told that no one knew who the kid was, that he was hanging around the studio when the song arrived and they let him demo it. Phillips decided to find someone else to record the song.

"What about the kid with the sideburns?" said Marion Keisker. Pause for commercial.

Elvis was called that same Saturday afternoon, and he rushed to the studio. Phillips played the demo for him. Elvis sang it, and it was ridiculous. He tried again, then again, but it was still ridiculous. Phillips gave up on "Without You" and suggested that Elvis try "Rag Mop," a song written by Johnnie Lee Wills (Bob Wills's brother) and Deacon Anderson. Wills had had a Top Ten country hit with it in 1950, on the Bullet label. The same year, the Ames Brothers had had a Number One pop hit with it, and Lionel Hampton had had a Top Ten R&B hit with

Best Wishes
Elvis Presley

it. It seemed an easy song (the lyrics are impressively dumb), but again Elvis was awkward and plain.

Sam, disturbed, asked Elvis just what in hell it was that he could sing. Oh, anything, Elvis replied. So do it, Sam said. And then, we are led to believe by the grooms of history, it poured forth, a crazy rush of disparate sounds: gospel (earlier in 1954, Elvis had almost joined the Blackwood Brothers, a gospel quartet that performed regularly on the WMPS *High Noon Roundup*), hard-core country, R&B, pop. For hours it went on, not a cool Apollonian eclecticism, but fevered glossolalia.

Sam called Winfield Scott Moore, better known as Scotty, the 22-year-old guitarist who had recorded with Doug Poindexter several weeks before. On Sunday, Independence Day, Elvis and Scotty met at Scotty's home, where they fooled with several recent country songs, such as Eddy Arnold's "I Really Don't Want To Know" and Hank Snow's "I Don't Hurt Anymore," both recent hits on RCA-Victor, and a few of singer Billy Eckstine's MGM sides. After a few hours, bass-player Bill Black, Scotty's neighbor, who had also played at Doug Poindexter's session, dropped in. He was not impressed, but the next evening, July 5, Black found himself in the Sun studio with Phillips, Presley, and Moore. It was Sam's idea for Scotty and Bill not to bring the rest of the Starlite Wranglers with them—no fiddle, no steel guitar. Sam had a different kind of country session in mind.

The first recording of "Blue Moon of Kentucky" was never released legally. (In 1975 Bobcat Records, a Dutch label, bootlegged the tape and included it in the album *Good Rocking Tonight*.) The version that was issued was recorded either the same night or the next night. Although this piece of history is clouded, it seems likely that the released version of "Blue Moon of Kentucky" was cut the same night as the version that caused Sam Phillips to utter, "Hell, that's different. That's a pop song now, Little Vi. That's *good.*" (Those words can be heard in *Good Rocking Tonight*.) They were in the groove then, touching tongues with the philosophers' stone Sam was seeking, and it's difficult to imagine their calling it a night at that moment of celebration.

"Blue Moon of Kentucky" as released in Elvis's first record, Sun 209, is surer, tougher than the earlier take. Like a young boxer after his first professional knockout, Presley is dizzy with the confirmation of his prowess. "Blue Moon of Kentucky" is daring to the point of mania. It is Elvis walking on steel blades, through orange-white flames, invincible with the knowledge he sees in Sam's eyes, hears in his own voice, and feels in his own flushed skin; the knowledge that right now, this moment, he, Elvis Aron Presley, is the greatest singer in Memphis and the universe. Nothing, not sex, not the eyes of bank-tellers, would ever again disarm with its mystery.

I think Elvis Presley will never be solved. It is strange enough that at the time of his first recordings, Elvis declared his idol to be Dean Martin, the 37-year-old Italian pop singer from Steubenville, Ohio, but to hear him at an August 22, 1957, press conference proclaim Pat Boone to be "undoubtedly the finest voice out now," and call Patti Page and Kay Starr his favorite female singers—this is modestly terrifying, a wild illogic.

Elvis never revealed himself. He died on August 16, 1977, at the age of 42. For all his fame and celebrity, he remains as mysterious and mythic as Homer. Possessed, estranged, then dead. Less than a month before Elvis died, a paperback book was published: *Elvis: What Happened?* by Red West, Sonny West, and Dave Hebler (three former Presley bodyguards), as told to Steve Dunleavy. It's an ill-written book, but a valuable one, shocking and ninety-percent correct.

The wonder will never die. There was more mystery, more power, in Elvis, singer of "Danny Boy," than in Bob Dylan, utterer of hermetic ironies. It is the sheer, superhuman tastelessness of Elvis that shakes the mind. In 1965, as Western civilization lay on its tummy peeking over the brink at the rapids of psilocybin and "(I Can't Get No) Satisfaction," Elvis, for all the world to see, was hopping about singing "Do the Clam." And the same week "Do the Clam" was released, Dean Martin came out with "Send Me the Pillow You Dream On," a Hank Locklin country hit from 1958. A few years later people began speaking of the revolutionary pop-country fusion wrought by the Byrds and Bob Dylan. Could Bob Dylan do the Clam? I bet Dino could.

After "Blue Moon of Kentucky," Elvis and the boys cut "That's All Right," a song originally recorded by Mississippi-born bluesman Ar-

ELVIS PRESLEY

The first feature article on Elvis appeared in the September 1955 issue of Country Song Roundup. *"There's no doubt about it,"* concluded the anonymous writer, *"this youngster is a real 'Folk Music Fireball'."*

thur Crudup, also known as Big Boy Crudup, for Victor in 1946. As Elvis performed it, it was no more a blues song, and no less a country song, than "Blue Moon of Kentucky." Where Bill Haley's versions of R&B songs were playfully mimetic, Elvis's were creative. He had no restraining concept of commercialism. Not yet, at least.

Elvis's first record, "Blue Moon of Kentucky" c/w "That's All Right," was released on July 19, 1954. Sam Phillips took a copy of the record to Dewey Phillips, the disk-jockey who hosted the *Red Hot and Blue* show at WHBQ, and he broadcast "That's All Right." Listeners called in their enthusiastic reactions. At WHHM disk-jockey Sleepy Eye John began spinning "Blue Moon of Kentucky." The record took off, and as the weeks passed, "That's All Right" became the Number One country record in Memphis.

That is when rockabilly became fact, and Elvis its avatar. On September 25, Elvis's second record was issued, a coupling of "Good Rockin' Tonight" (the 1947 Roy Brown song) and "I Don't Care If the Sun Don't Shine," written by Mack David, author of "Bibbidi Bobbidi Boo" and "*La Vie en Rose.*" Elvis made his debut on the Opry, as a guest in Hank Snow's segment. He sang both sides of his first single. After the show, Jim Denny, the boss of the Opry Artists Bureau (today he manages Cedarwood Publishing in Nashville), told Elvis he should go back to driving a truck. Elvis cried all the way back to Memphis.

On October 16, Presley played the Louisiana Hayride, where he went over so well that he was brought back the following week to become a regular performer.

The third Elvis record, released on January 8, 1955, was "Milkcow Blues Boogie," originally cut by Kokomo Arnold on Decca in 1935 and subsequently done by several country artists: Cliff Bruner (Decca, 1937), Johnnie Lee Wills (Decca, 1941), and Moon Mullican (King, 1946). The flip was "You're a Heartbreaker," a strong country weeper that was closer to a honky-tonk performance than any of Elvis's other Sun sides.

In "Milkcow Blues Boogie," it is obvious that Elvis is no longer innocent of commercial affectations. After a well-rehearsed false start, Elvis, in a voice that foreshadowed every black-and-white beatnik

Bill Monroe

★★★★ *Roanoke*
★★★★ *Cheyenne*

This is a must for them what likes good instrumental records, with the pickin' on both sides excellent. (**Decca 29406**)

Morgan Sisters

★★★★ *You Play Fiddlesticks*
★★★ *Evergreen*

Fiddlesticks is a fast tune well-sung by the girls who might have a big one this time. (**King 3913**)

Elvis Presley

★★★★★ *Milkcow Blues Boogie*
★★★★ *You're A Heartbreaker*

Two excellent sides by one of the bright newcomers in the country fields. (**Sun U-140**)

Marvin Rainwater

★★★★ *I Gotta Go Get My Baby*
★★★ *Daddy's Glad You Came Home*

Marvin does a top job on *Baby* with the Ridge Riders doing some fancy pickin' on both sides of this release. (**Coral 61342**)

Fred Rose

★★★★ *A New Flame*
★★ *Old Man Of The Sea*

Fred renews an old romance, and gets off a real good record. *Old Man* is just along for the ride. (**MGM K-11909**)

Record reviews from the April 1955 issue of Country & Western Jamboree.

movie of the late fifties, says, "Hold it, fellas. That don't move. Let's get real, real gone." It was the "Rock Around the Clock" syndrome, Elvis's first plunge into schmaltz.

"I'm Left, You're Right, She's Gone," written by Bill Taylor and Sun steel-guitarist Stan Kesler, and "Baby Let's Play House," recorded by Arthur Gunter on Excello earlier in the year, comprised the fourth single, issued on April 1, 1955. (Bill Taylor later revealed that his song was based on a Campbell's Soup advertisement, and that he wrote it while taking a bath.) For the first time, one of Presley's records hit the national country charts—"Baby Let's Play House" rose to the Number Ten position. As "Baby Let's Play House" was high on the charts, Elvis's last Sun disk was issued: "Mystery Train," an R&B song Junior Parker had cut for Sun in 1953, and "I Forgot To Remember To Forget," written by Charlie Feathers and Stan Kesler. In "Mystery Train" Scotty Moore showed the influence of Merle Travis. His guitar break toward the end of the record is an echo of the licks used by Travis in his 1946 "Sixteen Tons." The record became a double-barrelled hit, rising to the Number One position on the country charts. Elvis Presley, rock-and-roll madman, had the best-selling country record in the nation: The year 1955 belonged to Elvis Presley and *Blackboard Jungle.*

Late in 1955, Elvis signed with RCA-Victor. On January 5, 1956, in Nashville, Elvis cut his first sides for his new label. Now, in addition to Scotty and Bill and drummer D. J. Fontana (who had joined the group early in 1955), Nashville cats were involved: guitarist Chet Atkins, pianist Floyd Cramer, vocal group the Jordanaires. Elvis's first RCA-Victor recording, "Heartbreak Hotel," was released in February 1956. It became the Number One song on both the country and the pop charts.

"Heartbreak Hotel" was a superlative rockabilly song, full of austerity, sex, and stone-hard rhythm. The story of "Heartbreak Hotel" is this: Mae Boren Axton, songwriter and Hank Snow's P.R. lady, was shown a newspaper clipping by her friend Tommy Durden, another songwriter. The clipping reported a suicide by a young man who had left a one-line note: "I walk a lonely street." Axton and Durden wrote the song around the line and made a tape of it within a half hour. The song was offered to the Wilburn Brothers, who declined it.

For the next two years, Elvis continued to cut strong rockabilly for RCA-Victor: "Hound Dog," originally done by Willie Mae Thornton on Peacock in 1952 and covered by Tommy Duncan (formerly lead singer with Bob Wills) on Intro in 1953; "Don't Be Cruel," written for Elvis by Otis Blackwell (the demos Blackwell made, at Charlie Brave's Allegro studio in the basement of 1650 Broadway in New York City, were masterworks; all the vocal fillips and rhythmic heat of "Don't Be Cruel," "Great Balls of Fire," "Fever," and other hits were copied directly from Blackwell's demos); "Jailhouse Rock"; "Hard Headed Woman." Elvis sometimes reached beyond the usual sources; "Love Me Tender" was taken from the traditional ballad "Aura Lee."

With each new session, Elvis grew further from rockabilly. By the time he was drafted into the army in 1958, the golden days of rockabilly had passed.

As all things that contain more creativity than formula, more emotion than intellect, rockabilly cannot be precisely defined. As the word implies, rockabilly is hillbilly rock-and-roll. It was not a usurpation of black music by whites because its soul, its pneuma, was white, full of

---

HE HATES EVLIS

I'm an "I Hate Elvis" fan, and I'm positive no human being can make me change my mind.

If anyone can give me one good reason why I should like him, I will personally apologize.

5413 Franklin Ave.
New Orleans, La.

A future politician blows his cover in a 1959 issue of Dig.

the redneck ethos. When Elvis cut Big Boy Crudup's "That's All Right," he was no more usurping black culture than Wynonie Harris was usurping white culture when he cut country singer Hank Penny's "Bloodshot Eyes" three years before. Presley's version of "That's All Right" is better than the original, just as Harris's version of "Bloodshot Eyes" is better than its original. Think about it. Elvis has had more Number One R&B hits than Chuck Berry.

There was an affinity between rockabilly and black music of the 1940s and '50s, as there had been an affinity between Western swing and black music of the 1920s and '30s. But it was not, really, more than an affinity. Of the 16 known titles Elvis recorded as a Sun artist, 5 were derived from R&B records: "That's All Right," "Good Rockin' Tonight," "Milkcow Blues Boogie," "Baby Let's Play House," and "Mystery Train." (Two of these, in turn, were derived to a certain extent from country records: Arthur Gunter's "Baby Let's Play House" from Eddy Arnold's 1951 hit "I Want To Play House with You," and Junior Parker's "Mystery Train" from the Carter Family's 1930 "Worried Man Blues.") During his Sun years, as during the decades since, Elvis derived the bulk of his music from country and pop sources.

What blackness there was in rockabilly in no way constituted an innovation in country music. The black enculturation in the music of old-timers such as Jimmie Rodgers and Bob Wills was far greater, far deeper. Nor was there much of a technical nature in rockabilly that country music had not known before. The slap-bass technique, one of the watermarks of classic rockabilly, can be heard in country records of the pre-War era; for example, hear bassist Ramon DeArmon in the Light Crust Doughboys' 1938 Vocalion record "Pussy, Pussy, Pussy." The echo effect heard in many Sun rockabilly recordings had been used, less subtly, by Wilf Carter in his Victor records of the 1930s, and by Eddy Arnold in his 1945 "Cattle Call." (The unique echo sound of the Sun studio was achieved through the use of a tape-loop delay and a 7½-ips, instead of the more advanced 15-ips, two-track recorder. The added echo effect heard in Scotty Moore's guitar relied on a custom-built amplifier, made in Cairo, Illinois, by a man named Ray Butts. Moore got the second amp that Butts built; the first went to Chet

The low cost of rockabilly.

Atkins, the third to Carl Perkins, and the fourth to Roy Orbison. When he ceased working with Elvis in September 1957, Moore put the amp in a closet. Several closets later he withdrew it at Carl Perkins's request and plugged it in for one of Carl's Mercury sessions early in 1975.)

What made rockabilly such a drastically new music was its spirit, a thing that bordered on mania. Elvis's "Good Rockin' Tonight" was not merely a party song, but an invitation to a holocaust. Junior Parker's "Mystery Train" was an eerie shuffle; Elvis's "Mystery Train" was a demonic incantation. Country music in recent years had not known such vehement emotion, nor had black music. Rockabilly was the face of Dionysos, full of febrile sexuality and senselessness; it flushed the skin of new housewives and made pink teenage boys reinvent themselves as flaming creatures.

Although Elvis was the avatar, the unforgettable boy-daddy of rockabilly, there were others. In Memphis, and across the South, burning ever North, they drove country music berserk.

Ray Harris, 1973.

Carl Perkins's first record,
cut in December 1954.

Carl Lee Perkins was born on a welfare-supported tenant farm near Tiptonville, Tennessee, on April 9, 1932, the second of three brothers. His early years were spent on a plantation in Lake County, Tennessee, where his family were the sole white sharecroppers. In 1945, the Perkins family relocated in Bemis, where Carl began working as a laborer in a battery plant, then at a bakery in nearby Jackson.

In 1945 Carl won a talent show in Bemis. He taught his brothers, Jay B. and Clayton, to play guitars, and together the three performed locally as the Perkins Brothers Band.

Late in 1953, after he and his Mississippi-born wife, Valda Crider, moved to Parkview Courts, a government-subsidized housing project in Jackson, Carl sent demo tapes to various record companies in Nashville and New York. In December 1954, after a few unsuccessful attempts, Perkins had an audience with Sam Phillips at Sun. Several weeks later, in February of 1955, Sam issued Carl's first record on the Flip label (a Sun affiliate): "Movie Magg," which Carl had authored in 1945, and "Turn Around," a straight country piece.

52

With "Movie Magg," it became immediately apparent that Perkins was a consummate rock guitarist, given to rapid-fire high-note runs on his Les Paul Gibson. The Flip record got an impressive disk-jockey response in Memphis, as had Elvis's records during the previous seven months, and Sam signed Carl on as a regular Sun artist.

During the next years, until Carl left Sun in 1958, he had only seven singles released, or less than two a year. This small number of releases is odd in light of the fact that four of these records were country hits, and three of these four crossed to the pop charts. One of them, "Blue Suede Shoes," was a Top Ten hit on the country, pop, and R&B charts in 1956. Most likely Carl's records were overpressed in anticipation of another hit the magnitude of "Blue Suede Shoes."

Like Elvis, Carl Perkins sometimes used black material, as in his 1957 "Matchbox," a hard-edged version of Blind Lemon Jefferson's 1927 "Matchbox Blues" (which had been recorded by several country acts before Perkins: Larry Hensely in 1934, Joe Shelton in 1935, Roy Shaffer in 1939, Roy Newman and His Boys also in 1939, and the

PEEPLES MUSIC PUBLISHING CO.

917 LAIRD ST.   PASADENA, TEXAS

February 11, 1956

Sun Record Co., Inc.,

706 Union,

Memphis, Tenn.

                    Hi Lo Pub. Co.
                    Sun Record No. 234- By Carl Perkins
             Re.-"BLUE SUEDE SHOES"
Gentlemen:

This letter is to inform you that the song entitled,

"BLUE SUEDE SHOES" was officially published by Peeples

Music Pub. Co., 917 Laird St., Pasadena, Texas and cleared

through BMI on the date of August 22, 1955.

At the present time I hold the copyright to said song, and

the one of the same title, theme and tune which you just

recently released is so similar in every detail, that I

could not possibly release the one I have in my catalogue.

The writers feel that the song belongs to them and I am sure

that if you knew the reasons why they make their claims, that

you would be interested.

We would prefer to make an amicable settlement regarding the

publishing rights to this song; but we do feel that the song

belongs to us.

Please let me hear from you immediately regarding this matter.

                    Yours truly,

                    Curt Peeples.

                    Peeples Music Pub. Co.

February 15, 1956

Mr. Curt Peeples
Peeples Music Publishing Company
917 Laird Street
Pasadena, Texas

Dear Mr. Peeples:

We have your letter dated February 11th, and postmarked February 14th.

While we can appreciate your concern if you have a song of the same
title in your catalogue, we can assure you that it would be an amazing
artistic coincidence if there should be the duplication you speak of
between your copyrighted composition and the "BLUE SUEDE SHOES" that
Sun Record Company, Inc., has recorded.

The song recorded and released on Sun record #234 is a joint work of
two of our artists, Johnny Cash and Carl Perkins and was virtually
composed, over a period of several months, in our studios.

As you know, titles alone cannot be copyrighted, and many songs of
identical title can be composed, copyrighted, recorded and published
without any infringement of one another's rights.

We have no desire to intrude on anyone's rights and interests, and if
you wish to furnish us with a lead sheet of the composition that you
have copyrighted, we shall be glad to have an impartial professional
lead sheet man run a comparison of the melodies. Again we say, however,
that should any appreciable similarity be shown, it would be a surprising
coincidence, as we know under what circumstances the Sun recorded song
"BLUE SUEDE SHOES" was composed and written.

With kindest regards, we are,

Appreciatively,
SUN RECORD COMPANY, Inc.

Sam C. Phillips,
President

SCP:mk

Sam Phillips's reply.

A 1956 letter contesting the rights to "Blue Suede Shoes." (Left)

*He reached in his pocket
and he flashed a quart.*

Shelton Brothers in 1947). Unlike Elvis, however, Perkins was a consummate songwriter who was at his best in stuff such as the 1956 "Dixie Fried," a torrent of whiskey and violence, and the 1957 "Put Your Cat Clothes On" (unreleased until 1971), an anthem of redneck rock.

From Sun, Perkins went to Columbia, where he tried to recapture the success of "Blue Suede Shoes" with a series of wardrobe-rock contrivances: "Pink Pedal Pushers" and "Levi Jacket" in 1958, "Pointed Toe Shoes" in 1959. In 1963 he went to Decca. After Decca he signed with Dollie, an independent Nashville label, and in 1968 he returned to Columbia, where he stayed till 1973, when he joined Mercury, with whom he released only one album and a handful of singles.

COUNTRY

I believe in an ultimate and absolute rhythm.
  —Ezra Pound
    Sonnets and Ballate of Guido Cavalcanti

He who controls rhythm / controls.
  —Charles Olson,
    "Against Wisdom as Such"

It was three o'clock in the morning, and the master bedroom of Graceland was still. Elvis Presley lay in his orange silk pajamas, dreaming. It was the same old dream. He strode through Tupelo along Highway 78 in the late afternoon, toward the home of Mary. He had not seen her since that sexy, ruinous morning in 1955, and he was happy as he turned the corner onto Fourth; there was the house, where she waited in magic underwear. Suddenly he knew he was walking without shoes and socks. Pleasance became dread, and he flushed with panic. He would go across town, where in this dream his mother lived, and there get shoes and socks. If he hurried, there was time. He took a shortcut through a backyard he recognized, but he was soon lost, running barefoot and scared through strange, derisive streets, until he came to a meadow like none he had ever seen, and afternoon became night and the meadow became endless and he screamed.

The white telephone at Elvis's bedside was ringing. He reached and pressed a small silver button on the box of walnut and black glass that sat near the phone. Its dark face lighted, 3:07. Beneath the time, in smaller lines, was the date, November 23, 1976. He lifted the receiver. It was Robert Loyd, a Graceland security guard, calling from the guardpost downstairs. There was trouble.

At the gate Jerry Lee Lewis leaned against his 1976 Lincoln Continental. He held a .38-caliber derringer, and he was drunk. He had come to liberate Elvis, to speak with Elvis, to murder Elvis, to sing with Elvis. He demanded Elvis come to the gate. Then he demanded he be brought in to Elvis. He waved the gun and yelled curses. His eyes tightened with wrath, and he shouted for Elvis. Loyd was scared, and he asked Elvis's advice. Ignore him, Elvis said.

Jerry Lee raved on, and Loyd called the cops. Memphis patrolman B. J. Kirkpatrick arrived to find Lewis sitting in his car, holding the derringer at his knee. The trigger was cocked. He was arrested and charged with public drunkenness and carrying a pistol, then released on $250 bond pending a hearing the next morning. He did not appear in court for the hearing, and a warrant was issued for his arrest. Later in the day the warrant was dismissed by Judge Albert H. Boyd at the request of Lewis's lawyer. The night after the disturbance Jerry Lee entered Doctors Hospital for treatment of peptic ulcers and influenza.

Less than 24 hours before his arrest at Graceland, Lewis was arrested at a street corner near his home in Collierville, east of Memphis. After driving his 13-year-old daughter, Phoebe, to school, he overturned his $46,000 Rolls-Royce. He was charged with reckless driving, driving while intoxicated, and driving without a license. Collierville police chief, H. A. Goforth, Jr., said Lewis was given a Breathalizer test, but it proved negative. The police were baffled by this thaumaturgy, and could do nothing but free him on $250 bail pending a hearing.

After this arrest Jerry Lee told a reporter he resented that the press treated Elvis as royalty and him, Jerry Lee, as white trash. "You all hate my guts or something," he said. "I'm no angel, but I'm a pretty nice guy." Hours later he waited, gun cocked, outside the big house on Elvis Presley Boulevard.

That Monday night, not long after Jerry Lee had magicked the Collierville breathalizer, his father, Elmo Lewis, was arrested near Robinsonville, Mississippi, and charged with speeding and driving while intoxicated. He refused to take an alcohol-content test and was placed in Tunica County Jail. On Tuesday morning he was released on $300 bond pending a hearing later in the day. The elder Lewis fled across the state line to Tennessee.

On September 30, a few hours before his forty-first birthday, Jerry Lee shot Norman "Butch" Owens, his bass player, in the upper chest with a .357 magnum. Owens survived, and Jerry Lee told police he thought the gun was empty. A hearing was set for nine o'clock, October 14, but Jerry did not appear.

The week after he shot his bass player, Jerry Lee was arrested at his home and charged with disorderly conduct. Neighbors had complained that Lewis was shouting obscenities at them.

There had always been legal fires. Until 1975 Jerry Lee kept an office in Memphis: Jerry Lee Lewis Enterprises, Inc., Suite 805, 3003 Airways Boulevard. But one night he blasted 25 holes through his office door with a .45 automatic, and he was asked to leave.

Back in the early sixties, before San Francisco first uttered the word *psychedelic,* Jerry Lee and his band, the Memphis Beats, were arrested at a motel in Grand Prairie, Texas, and charged with possession of 700 amphetamine capsules; 200 were for the band, 500 for Jerry Lee. In March 1975, after San Francisco last uttered the word *psychedelic,* federal narcotics agents boarded Lewis's Convair 640 at the Denver airport (Jerry Lee and the boys had just arrived from Canada) and took what a government spokesman called "a substantial amount of drugs." Lewis claimed it was a set-up. The dope was confiscated, but no arrest was made.

Believe it: Jerry Lee Lewis is a creature of mythic essence, a Set, a Baptist Dionysos. He is the heart of redneck rock-and-roll and, maybe, the greatest country singer alive. Talk about rock-and-roll depravados: Jerry Lee makes them all look like Wayne Newton. Talk about honky-tonk heroes: Next to Jerry Lee, they're a bunch of frat-party pukers. "I was born feet first, been rockin' ever since," he'll tell you if he's in a good mood. His vassals and kin will tell you more: Jerry Lee can out-drink, out-dope, out-fight, out-cuss, out-shoot, and out-fuck any man in the South. He is the last American wild man, *homo agrestis americanus ultimus,* and his everyday deeds are the stuff of Don Siegel movies. "Just don't get too close to him and you won't get hurt," said Waylon Jennings. In all ways he is a lord of excess. "I've seen him eat four steaks and then eat again in a couple of hours," said his sister Linda Gail.

In 1975 Donnie Fritts (also known as the Elegant Alabama Leaning Man), a Nashville songwriter and actor in several Peckinpah movies, wrote a song for Jerry Lee called "A Damn Good Country Song." Jerry Lee cut it, and Mercury released it as a single.

NICK TOSCHES

Well, I took enough pills for the whole damn town;
Jerry Lee Lewis drank enough whiskey to lift any
*   ship off of the ground.*
I'll be the first to admit it;
I sure wish that these people would quit it,
Cuz it's tough enough to straighten up when
*   they won't leave you alone.*
My life would make a damn good country song. *

He was born on September 29, 1935, in Ferriday, Louisiana, the second son of Elmo and Mary Ethel Lewis. The older son, Elmo, Jr., was killed in a car wreck at the age of nine. After Jerry Lee came two daughters, Frankie Jean and Linda Gail. Frankie Jean says her daddy, a carpenter, helped build Angola Prison Farm; she says Jerry Lee started playing piano in 1944, and that "Silent Night" was the first song he could play straight through. In the fall of 1949, Ferriday's Ford dealer presented a show in his parking lot to hail the new line of cars. Jerry joined the band and sang and played piano for 20 minutes. He raped the down-home crowd with his version of "Drinkin' Wine Spo-Dee-O-Dee," which had been an R&B hit twice that year, first by Stick McGhee and then by Wynonie Harris. The crowd dropped a glorious $13 in Jerry's kitty, and he decided to go professional.

The next year, Jerry worked at the Blue Cat Night Club in Natchez. On Saturdays he had a 20-minute radio program at WNAT in the same city. His sister Linda Gail recalls that he hitched to New Orleans to make a record, but none was made. He brought home his report card: 29 F's.

After high school, he attended Southwestern Bible Institute, a school of the Assembly of God in Waxahachie, Texas. (In 1963 the Institute changed its name to Southwestern Assemblies of God College. According to its Bulletin, the College "embraces standards of living and conduct that are the same as those generally accepted by the Pentecostal

*"A Damn Good Country Song" by Donnie Fritts. Copyright © 1975 by Combine Music Corporation. Used by permission.

60

churches in America. These are characterized by clean conduct and conversation, modest apparel in dress, high standards of moral life, and a deep consecration and devotion in spiritual life.") Jerry Lee was expelled for ravaging "My God Is Real" during a performance in chapel.

Back in Ferriday, he became a door-to-door seller of vacuum cleaners. He quit in 1952 when he got a regular job at the Wagon Wheel in Natchez, drumming in a trio led by Paul Whitehead, a blind pianist. Sometimes Whitehead switched to trumpet or accordion, and Jerry was then allowed to play piano.

Jerry Lee first married when he was 14. The marriage, to Dorothy Barton, lasted little more than a year. In 1954 he married Jane Mitcham of Natchez, and on November 2 of that year his first son, Jerry Lee, Jr., was born. (On November 13, 1973, Jerry Lee, Jr., was killed in a car wreck near Cockrum, Mississippi. He had spent part of the year in a nuthouse, which he attributed to the evil effects of marijuana upon his brain. A few weeks before his death, he was saved at an Assembly of God revival.)

Soon after his son was born, Lewis went to Shreveport to audition for the Louisiana Hayride, a show broadcast by KWKH and patterned after the Grand Ole Opry. The Hayride's newest star was Elvis Presley, who had made his debut there in October. Lewis recorded an audition disk for Slim Whitman, who was boss of a Hayride package tour. Whitman listened to the record. "I Don't Hurt Anymore," a then-current country hit by Hank Snow, was on one side; "If I Ever Needed You" was on the other. He handed the disk to Lewis and said, "Don't call me; I'll call you." Jerry Lee remembers Whitman as "that old nub-fingered sonofabitch."

Jerry Lee came to Sun Records in Memphis early in 1956. Sam Phillips, who owned Sun, had recently sold Elvis to RCA-Victor for $35,000 (which he still truculently denies ever regretting), and he was in the market for a new punk prodigy.

Lewis's first record was a coupling of "Crazy Arms," the Ray Price hit that was still on the charts when Jerry Lee cut it in the fall of 1956, and "End of the Road," an original song. He did not pursue writing in subsequent years (of the several hundred titles he has cut in the past 21 years, only five bear his signature: "End of the Road," "High School Confidential," and "Lewis Boogie" on Sun, and "Lincoln Limousine," an odd song about John Kennedy's death, and "He Took It like a Man" on Smash); however, in "End of the Road" Jerry Lee proved himself a masterful evoker of lurid mood and dark thirst, and it is precious, and poetically just, to look at the song as a statement of purpose, an existential anthem of the career to follow:

> *Well, the way is dark,*
> *Night is long,*
> *I don't care if I ever get home:*
> *I'm waitin' at the end of the road!*

Radio station WHBQ premiered Jerry Lee's first record. In July 1954, the station had premiered Elvis's first record.

Jerry Lee had the two biggest hits of Sun's history: "Whole Lot of Shakin' Going On" and "Great Balls of Fire." The former was written

COUNTRY

The Killer arrives, 1956.

Jerry Lee Lewis's first EP,
released in October, 1957.

63

by Dave Williams and Sunny David and first recorded by the Com-
modores in 1955 on Dot. Later that year, the song was covered by Roy
Hall, a *meshuganer* country singer and piano-player from Stone Gap,
Virginia, who recorded for Decca, and by Dolores Fredericks, who also
recorded for Decca. Jerry Lee learned the song from Johnny Littlejohn,
a drummer who sometimes played at the Wagon Wheel in Natchez
with Paul Whitehead's group. "Whole Lot of Shakin' Going On" was
cut by Lewis early in 1957 and released on April 15, his second record.

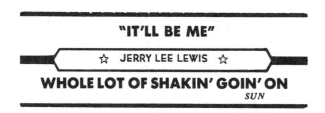

"IT'LL BE ME"

☆ JERRY LEE LEWIS ☆

WHOLE LOT OF SHAKIN' GOIN' ON
SUN

On August 31 it hit the Number One slots in both the country and R&B
charts (only one other person in the history of popular music has had
Number One hits in both of these markets: Elvis), and in September
it hit Number Two in the pop charts. In October the record appeared
in the British charts, where it soon reached Number Eight. In the end,
the record sold six million copies worldwide. Jerry Lee sang it on
American Bandstand; Dick Clark recalls that Lewis was the only guest
he encountered who refused to lip-sync. (In many ways, Jerry Lee is a
purist, or more precise, a primitivist. "I don't like no overdubbin'," he
has said. "When you're makin' love to a woman, ya can't go back in
and overdub.")

Recorded in the fall of 1957 and released on November 3, "Great
Balls of Fire" peaked in January 1958, when it was Number One
country, Number Two pop, Number Five R&B, and Number One in
Britain. The song was written for Lewis by Otis Blackwell (who had
written "Don't Be Cruel" and "All Shook Up" for Elvis, and whom
Jerry Lee described as "a little colored fellow in a derby hat"), and it
was intended that Jerry Lee would perform the song in the Warner

Brothers film *Jamboree,* his movie debut. Directed by Roy Lockwood, and featuring Lewis, Fats Domino, Count Basie, Carl Perkins, Slim Whitman, Frankie Avalon, and others, *Jamboree* was released in December 1957. Lobby cards described the film as "a fast-spinning love story behind the scenes of today's brand new kind of Tin Pan Alley!"

"Great Balls of Fire" was a fine and sleazy record, the yell of a tribe sloughing its senses, examining its crotch as if for the first time. The day the record was released, the Commies fired their second silly Sputnik, a half-ton ball circling 900 miles up, a dog panting fearfully within, stranger than any Egyptian glyph. Eisenhower lay numb and still from a stroke; Nixon, large wet cow liver of a human, ruled. Charlie Starkweather, 5-foot-2 "red-headed peckerwood" (the words of his confession), thrashed and skidded through Nebraska and Wyoming murdering and murdering and murdering. How many times did Starkweather gnash and grin with sexy delight as "Great Balls of Fire" crackled from his car radio?

By 1958 Jerry Lee Lewis was on top. Of all the rock-and-roll creatures, he projected the most hellish persona. He was feared more than the rest, and hated more too. Preachers railed against him, mothers smelled his awful presence in the laundry of their daughters, and young boys coveted his wicked, wicked ways.

My friend Michael Bane grew up in Memphis in the fifties, and he has tenebrious memories of the Killer's role in local society.

"There was this dive, I mean a real dive, called Hernando's Hideaway. It was located just south of town, toward the Mississippi line—a great two-story house, all black. When we drove by, my parents would snort and say, 'That's where people like Jerry Lee Lewis play.' My mother was real adamant about how, essentially, he was the garbage of the earth. She couldn't stand him; she couldn't stand thinking about him.

"He kind of balanced things out in Memphis. He made Elvis acceptable. Elvis tried to be good. Folks could look at him and say, 'This is a good boy.' But Jerry Lee was always a shitkicker. There were always horror stories. There was always an aura of extreme violence to Jerry Lee."

Jerry Lee Lewis is the greatest song stylist in country music. (He himself will tell you there have been only three real stylists in the whole of music: Al Jolson, Jimmie Rodgers, and Jerry Lee Lewis.) A recording by Jerry Lee is as unmistakable as a passage by Faulkner. Bursting phrases recur throughout Jerry Lee's music. "Think about it!" he yells before a strafe-force barrage of ascending triplets. (Scholars, please note: The first "Think about it!" is found in "Foolish Kind of Man," in the 1971 album *Touching Home.*) Pindar would have loved it: *"Think about it!"* How similar to Faulkner, who while writing his third novel fell upon the word *indomitable* and for the rest of his days did not write a book without a handful of grand, truculent *indomitable*s. And Jerry Lee is permitted his vast liberties, as Faulkner was permitted his. Jerry Lee is the only country singer who can get away with yelling at his audience, referring to his musicians as motherfuckers, just as Faulkner got away with statements such as his description of a mule in *Flags in the Dust:* "Misunderstood even by that creature (the nigger who drives him) whose impulses and mental processes most closely resemble his." I also hold that William Faulkner and Jerry Lee Lewis possess the profoundest and most beautiful masteries of rhythm in this century. And, of course, to both, their whiskey and hawk-eye redneck ways.

The piano, the wife / gun of Jerry Lee's music, came late to country music. In 1775 John Behrent of Philadelphia made the first American piano, and in 1823 Jonas Chickering of Boston began the first steady manufacture of New World pianos. (He constructed them with cast-iron frames, to withstand the rigors of shipment in America.) In 1860 there were about 22,000 pianos in the States. The upright piano, the kind Jerry Lee played in his Ferriday home, was invented about 1800 and was first known as the *pianino* or *piano droit.* One of the first makers of uprights was an American, J. I. Hawkins of Philadelphia. Its smaller size and weight took it places where pianos had never been: bars, whorehouses, tent shows, and small homes. In it, Southern music found a new tool. One of the first Opry performers, Theron Hale (born about 1883 in Pikeville, Tennessee), used a piano in his band as early as 1926. Al Hopkins's Hill Billies, Dr. Bates's Possum Hunters, Ed Poplin, and other Opry acts of the late twenties also used pianos.

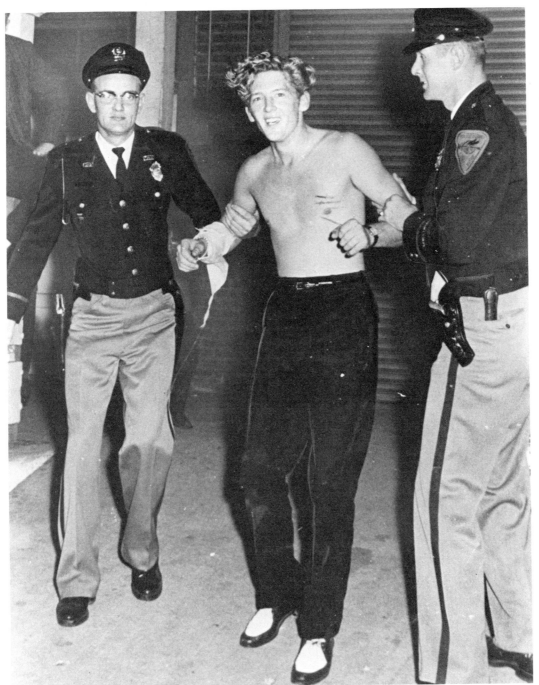

Go ye therefore, and teach all nations, baptizing them in the name of the Father, and of the Son, and of the Holy Ghost.

Two country pianists wrought influences on Jerry Lee: Moon Mullican and Del Wood. Mullican (his true first name was Aubrey) was born March 27, 1909, in Corrigan, Texas; he died New Year's Day, 1967, in Beaumont, Texas. He was the first country piano-player to record in a boogie-woogie style. Though the phrase didn't occur on record till 1928, when Clarence "Pinetop" Smith, a blues singer who was murdered at the age of 23, cut "Pinetop's Boogie Woogie," the style originated in the early twenties. Its father was Jimmy Yancey (1894–1951), who used the eight-to-the-bar pattern and improvised contrapuntally in both bass and treble. Yancey was not recorded until 1939, but he was the mentor of Meade Lux Lewis (1905–1964), whose 1927 "Honky Tonk Train Blues" was the first true boogie-woogie record. The style spread through the thirties, with Albert Ammons (1907–1949) and Pete Johnson (1904–1967) its most famed masters. By 1940 boogie-woogie was popular among white audiences, and Tommy Dorsey, the Andrews Sisters, Bob Crosby, Woody Herman, and others were having pop hits with songs like "Beat Me Daddy, Eight to a Bar" and "Boogie Woogie Bugle Boy." The first boogie-woogie country record was Johnny Barfield's "Boogie Woogie" in 1939. The Delmore Brothers coined a phrase when they cut "Hillbilly Boogie" in 1945.

Moon Mullican recorded with Cliff Bruner's band in the late thirties. Bruner: "When I left Milton Brown, I hired Moon as my piano man. Moon developed his own, he used to call it 'three-finger style.' And he didn't play very good when I hired him, but he developed into a fine piano man, terrific showman. Later on, he and I had a band together for a few years. Called it Cliff Bruner, Moon Mullican, and The Showboys."

In 1945 Mullican signed with King Records. There were hits: "New Pretty Blonde (New Jole Blon)" (1947), "I'll Sail My Ship Alone" (1950), "Mona Lisa" (1950), "Cherokee Boogie" (1951). Then for 10 years Moon was in the shadows; in 1961 he had one last hit, "Ragged But Right" on Starday. While performing at the Kansas City Auditorium in 1962, Moon had a heart attack (he weighed 275 pounds at the time). He continued to record, for Kapp and independent labels such as Hall and Spar. On the last day of 1966, Moon made a New Year's resolution to lay off pork chops. He died before the first day of 1967 ended.

Del Wood (shortened from Adelaide Hazelwood) was born February 22, 1920, in Nashville. She was an old-fashioned piano-player with a hard, clear barrelhouse style. Her first and only hit was "Down Yonder," a 1951 instrumental on the Tennessee label. The tune was an old one, written by New Orleans pianist L. Wolfe Gilbert in 1920 and performed by the Brown Brothers in the musical *Tip Top* that same year. Wood's version hit the pop charts first (it rose to Number Six), then crossed to the country charts, where it entered at Number Nine, but disappeared after one week. She made her Opry debut on February 23, 1952, and has performed regularly in the show since then. After leaving the Tennessee label in early 1953, Del recorded for Republic, then RCA-Victor. In her Chart album, *Are You from Dixie?*, recorded in the late sixties, she performed a thing called "Psychedelic Mockingbird," an original composition.

Jerry Lee loved Del's record of "Down Yonder," and when he first came to Nashville in the fifties, she was one of the few people who treated him with kindness. When he made his belated Opry debut, on

January 20, 1973, he interrupted his performance (the Nashville corpus held its breath in grim anxiety) and invited Del Wood onstage. She sat at the piano with him, and together they partied out "Down Yonder," then they embraced. In 1969 Bob Dylan had offered a song to Jerry Lee ("To Be Alone with You"), and Charles Conrad had brought a cassette of Jerry Lee's music to the moon aboard Apollo XII. Quotidian stuff: Jerry Lee misplaced Dylan's demo, looked to the full moon for a moment. But a chance to play piano with Del Wood—that was something! (The next October, John Lennon came backstage to Jerry Lee's dressing room at the Roxy in Los Angeles; he knelt gracefully and kissed Jerry Lee's foot. Jerry Lee looked down to see if his shoe-shine had been smarmed.) Jerry Lee also liked the work of Merrill Moore, the popular jazz pianist from Iowa who recorded "House of Blue Lights" (1953), "Down the Road Apiece" (1955), and other jazz-rockers for Capitol.

But the most important musical influence on Jerry Lee was Cecil Gant. Not much is known of him. He was a black pianist and singer, who was born in 1915 in Nashville and died in 1951 in New York City, apparently of liquor. He recorded from 1944 to 1951, for Gilt Edge, Bronze, Four Star, Sound, Bullet, Dot, Down Beat, Swing Time, Imperial, Decca, and National. His first release, "I Wonder," issued by Gilt Edge of Los Angeles in 1944, was a hit, and Gant remained a well-known and successful artist till his death.

Much of Cecil Gant's music was boogie-woogie, but it was wilder, tougher than the classic boogie styles. His "Nashville Jumps," recorded for Bullet in 1947, is one of the perfect party records.

> *Seen ya goin' up Cedar Street hill,*
> *I know you got your whiskey from Jack Daniel's still!*
> *Nashville really jumps, really jumps all night long;*
> *I'd rather be in Nashville than to be way back down home.*
> *Yeah, jump, Nashville!*

Before the last stanza, Gant yells, "Gimme another drink and I'll be all right!"

Some of Gant's records were what can only be called rock-and-roll. The most striking of these is "We're Gonna Rock," recorded in July 1950 in New York City for Decca. The piano introduction of "We're Gonna Rock" is indistinguishable from Jerry Lee's Sun style.

Jerry Lee was in his mid teens when Cecil Gant was recording his finest work. He was 15 when "We're Gonna Rock" was released, and its force still reverberates in the heart of his music.

It is not unlikely that Sam Phillips signed Lewis because he brought to mind black pianist Ike Turner, who had played in the classic Jackie Brenston rock sessions Phillips had produced in 1951. Elvis, the white boy who sang like he had a nigger's soul, was lost, over the lea, sold to RCA-Victor for $35,000. Here was a white boy who played piano like a crazy nigger; maybe history would repeat itself. It didn't.

Jerry Lee fell in the spring of 1958. Arriving for a tour of England in May, he was made victim of a seedy media-gale which tsk-wailed and screamed that his wife (he had married a third time), Myra Gail, was also his 13-year-old cousin. With his usual speed, Jerry responded to the British press: "Myra and I are legally married. It was my second marriage that wasn't legal. I was a bigamist when I was sixteen. I was fourteen when I was first married. That lasted a year; then I met Jane. One day she said she was goin' to have my baby. I was real worried. Her father threatened me, and her brothers were hunting with hide whips. So I married her just a week before my divorce from Dorothy. It was a shotgun wedding." Britain was not pleased. It was announced in the London *Times* of May 28 that the tour, which was to have lasted until June 29 and included appearances at 27 Rank theatres, had been canceled.

A curious fact is that not long before Lewis left for England, his cousin-wife had sued him for divorce. From the Associated Press, Memphis, March 11, 1958: "The wife of Jerry Lee Lewis, rock 'n' roll entertainer, filed for a divorce today." Through all this, J. W. Brown, Myra's 31-year-old daddy, played bass in Jerry Lee's band.

Jerry Lee and Myra Gail were belatedly divorced in the fall of 1970. (They had two children: Steve Allen, named for the man who was responsible for Lewis's TV debut, was born in 1959; Phoebe Allen was born in 1963. Steve Allen Lewis drowned in the family pool in 1962.) In court Myra testified that their marriage was "a nightmare." Jerry Lee was placed under court injunction "not to threaten, molest, or intimidate" his 26-year-old cousin. In October 1971, he wed Jaren Pate. They had one child, Lori Lee, born in 1972. In 1974 Jaren filed for legal separation.

The New York Times of May 29, 1958, was sinister: "Jerry Lee Lewis Back," as one might announce the return of a viral strain. In the same issue of the *Times* was an advertisement for the film *High School Confidential,* which opened the next day at the Loew's State in Times Square: "Exploding Tomorrow with Even More Shock!" Scenes were depicted: wielded switchblade, belly-to-belly kiss, punch-out.

High School Confidential was Lewis's second movie. Starring were Russ Tamblyn, John Drew Barrymore, Mamie Van Doren, and Charles Chaplin, Jr. Jack Arnold, the director, had previously made *With These Hands* (1950), *Girls in the Night* (1953), *It Came from Outer Space* (1953), *The Creature from the Black Lagoon* (1955), *Return of the Creature* (1955), and *The Incredible Shrinking Man* (1957). *High School Confidential* has since been renamed *Young Hellions.*

Lewis had cut the title song of *High School Confidential* on April 21, 1958, before his ruined English tour. Released on May 20, the record never broke the pop Top Twenty. The effects of the scandal were severe. In the June 9 issue of *Billboard,* a full-page advertisement appeared. "An Open Letter to the Industry from Jerry Lee Lewis" began, "Dear Friends: I have in recent weeks been the apparent center of a fantastic amount of publicity and of which none has been good. . . ."

But nothing was healed. "High School Confidential" was Jerry Lee's last appearance in the Top Ten of the country charts until 1968, and his last appearance, period, in the Top Twenty of both the pop and R&B charts. Six months earlier radio stations had held loud elections: Who's the King of rock 'n' roll? Elvis or Jerry Lee? (In many areas, such as that of WHB in Kansas City, Lewis had won two-to-one.) Now his price dropped to $500 a night, and disk-jockeys wouldn't play his records.

Jerry Lee Lewis, c. 1964.

Jerry Lee Lewis doing business as the Hawk, 1960.

Jerry Lee Lewis kept pumping. That word Faulkner loved: *indomitable.* In 1968 he rose anew with a series of country hits that started with "Another Place, Another Time," the best honky-tonk song of the sixties, for Smash. Of the Sun rockabilly triumvirate—Elvis, Carl Perkins, and Jerry Lee—he is the only one still making 101-proof rockabilly on a grand scale.

The mythology of Jerry Lee Lewis has a thousand devoted Hesiods. Since the beginning, Jerry demanded to close every show he appeared in. In 1958 Alan Freed insisted that Lewis precede Chuck Berry in a show. They still talk of that show, how Jerry Lee had the crowd screaming and rushing the stage, how he took a can of Zippo from his jacket pocket and doused his piano with one hand as the other hand banged out "Whole Lot of Shakin' Going On," how he set the piano aflame, his hands still riding the keys like a madman as the kids went finely and wholly berserk with the frenzy of it, and how Jerry Lee stalked backstage stinking of lighter fluid and wrath, turned to Chuck Berry, and said, real calm, as the sound of the kids going crazy and stamping and yelling for more shook the walls, "Follow *that,* nigger."

74

A record-company executive recalls another meeting between Jerry Lee and Chuck Berry. The executive was producing a concert in which both singers were to appear. Jerry Lee started a fight with Berry backstage; much drinking and aggravation followed. When the executive called for the curtains to be opened, there at center stage stood Jerry Lee, Chuck Berry, and Elmo Lewis. Chuck Berry was holding a knife to Jerry Lee's throat, and Pappy Lewis had the open end of a shotgun pressed to the base of Berry's skull. The audience uttered no sound.

There is said to have been a time when Jerry Lee's drummer, Morris "Tarp" Tarrant, was eager to have Jerry smoke marijuana, perhaps in the hope that it would soften the lines of his personality. On a night when there was much potent Jamaican dope circulating, Jerry Lee consented to try it. Tarp rolled a very fat joint, a thing of true Jerry Lee Lewis proportion, and Jerry sat with it, consuming its smoke in deep, strong sucks. All awaited the verdict, the birth of Jerry Lee, flower child, cherub of peace and soft colors. He rose. "Not bad," he said, then quickly swallowed five small pills, grabbed a fifth of Old Crow, and departed into the night.

Somewhere in the direst and scariest gut of Alabama, Jerry Lee was playing a honky-tonk. It was a gas-money date. Pick up some cash and split. Toward the beginning of the second set, a drunken, thick, red man encroached Jerry Lee. He was angry. "My wife's crazy about you," he said, motioning to a female dissolved in darkness and smoke and the blurred vision both men shared. "She bought every record you ever made. But I think you're a piece a shit, and you know what I just did? I went home and busted ever one of them records. Whatchoo think about that, boy?" Jerry Lee moved his face close to the drunk's, captured his pupils with his own, and in a voice neither loud nor soft, said, "Good, now she's gotta go out and buy 'em all over again."

There was a wife, one of them, whom Jerry Lee left sleeping in a Nashville motel room. He returned to the room moments before dawn. He carried a lighted cigar and a submachine gun. The wife was awakened in a novel way, as the wall above her head was shattered with metal.

Merle Haggard tells of his night with Jerry Lee in 1974. "We were in that little room at the bottom of the King of the Road in Nashville, and he had already busted some guy in the mouth that night, a guy who was a life-long fan of his. The guy was just in awe of Jerry Lee. I knew the guy, and he was a piano-player. This guy was sitting there watching Jerry Lee play and all of a sudden—BAK!—Jerry took his whiskey bottle and busted it in his face, cut the guy's face all up to pieces. I found Jerry Lee that next morning, about six o'clock. I had just heard about what he'd done and, well, I figured he was in one of those rare moods. He said, 'Well, let's go out and pick.' So we did."

A former employee of Mercury Records in New York tells of the night he was supposed to deliver Jerry Lee to the ABC TV studio to tape the *Dick Cavett Show.* Jerry Lee was very, very drunk. "Are you sure you want to do the show?" the employee kept asking him. And Jerry Lee kept nodding and falling back asleep. The limousine pulled up in front of the studio, 20 minutes before taping, and the employee shook Jerry Lee and his manager, Judd Phillips, awake. "Is this the bus depot?" they asked peering out at some private geometry of gin.

Writers have not had much success interviewing Jerry Lee. One night in Brooklyn in 1973, an editor of *Country Music* asked Jerry Lee a question. The interviewee responded by leaping across the table, breaking off the butt of his pint-bottle of Heaven Hill, and sticking the interviewer in the neck with it.

Armed, I attended a Jerry Lee Lewis recording session in Memphis. Pappy Lewis was there. On his way to the studio, Pappy had been chased down the highway by the Memphis police as he rushed along in Jerry Lee's white, custom-built Lincoln (1-FZ541) at a speed of 110 miles per hour. Pappy's reaction to his situation was ingenious. He increased his speed until he put enough distance between himself and the police so that he was invisible to them. Then he skidded the car to the side of the road, jumped in the back seat, and waited. The police arrived in a moment. "Glad you showed up, boys," Pappy said. "That crazy man drivin' this car was like to get us killed. When he saw your light flashin', he stopped the car and ran off into them trees there." The cops stared dully at the vacant driver's seat. "My son's Jerry Lee Lewis. He's makin' a record on Poplar Avenue, and I gotta be there. This is

Jerry Lee and his father, Elmo, 7 miles over Babylon, 1972.
Photo courtesy of Malcolm Temple.

his car. I'm in no condition to drive myself. How's about one you boys takin' me? Jerry be purty mad I don't git his car back to him." He was driven to the studio.

Earlier in the day, at Jerry Lee's office, the scene was something like this: Jerry was on the telephone, shouting. "He's gonna sue *me?* You tell that sonofabitch husband of yours that if he tries to sue me I'm gonna come over there and give him the biggest ass-whuppin' he ever got in his life." There were perhaps 12 other people in the room. Everyone was drunk, and a few were falling asleep as Jerry shouted into the phone. It was ten o'clock in the morning. For some reason, Jerry Lee was drinking bourbon and orange juice, a combination the color of wan excrement. "He's on a health kick," somebody suggested.

77

Pappy Lewis decided to try some orange juice in his bourbon, so he asked someone to give him the Tropicana container from Jerry's desk. Jerry Lee banged the hand with the receiver as it was about to touch the orange juice. From the wielded receiver, a woman's voice was faint and shrill: "What the fuck was that?" Jerry was indignant. "What the hell you doin' my orange juice?" A voice attached to the hand, a drunken voice, answered, "It's for your father." Jerry Lee returned the receiver to his ear. "Shoot. Tell him to go buy his own fuckin' orange juice. You still there, darlin'?"

At the recording session was a one-armed man named Paul. He introduced himself. "Mr. Lewis, you probably don't remember me—"

"Right," Jerry said.

Soon the one-armed man was very drunk, and he beat his wife, who seemed to be a short Indian. She left him, for good it seemed. The one-armed man said, "Fuck her." He approached a girl who sat quietly in a corner. "Hey, baby, what's shakin'?" He dangled his armless, folded sleeve in her face. The girl was repulsed. Judd Phillips, who had been sleeping, said to the one-armed man, "Watch it or I'll snitch the other one off." Jerry Lee laughed, low and dark. The girl ran from the studio.

Pappy Lewis seemed to be speaking in Hittite. Only Jerry could comprehend him, or perhaps he was merely faking. "You know you ain't supposed to drink." Pappy responded in Hittite and spilled an eight-ounce Dixie cup of whiskey into his lap, a deed he loudly regretted, in Hittite. With Pappy was the son of his girlfriend. The future son-in-law was about 30, drunk but not in the Hittite fashion. It surfaced that Pappy could not remember his fiancee's name, but he was sure the fiancee was mad with him. "Get a dime; call your mama," he said, in English, or something like it.

An obviously psychopathic youth with eyes the size of gull eggs ran about telling anyone he could catch, "I'm a writer for *TV Guide.* I write about country artisez. Did you ever hear of the Grateful Dead? They played at my wedding. My wife's a model. She poses for artisez. She poses naked: tits, hiney, everything. She makes more money than you and me both. I hired a private eye to follow her around all day, and he keeps a little book of all the people she fucks behind my back. He's very expensive."

A woman with bleached hair was referred to by all as "the curse of the family," a distinction of awesome implication.

A man dressed in black and carrying a bottle of Peter Pan Port introduced himself to the curse of the family. "Don't get fresh," she said, frequently. He was the drummer with Bobby and the Spotlites, the house band at Hernando's Hideaway. There was a pack of cigarettes sticking from each of his pockets. Every pack was open, and he smoked from them variously. Memphis session organist James Brown was in the studio. The drummer from Hernando's Hideaway saw him and screamed, "Oh, my God, don't tell me Jerry Lee's got spooks in his band!" The curse of the family applied lipstick.

Judd fell asleep on the floor. Jerry Lee gently kicked him awake and said, "Take out your teeth and I'll marry ya." Judd returned to sleep.

Through all this, Huey Meaux was trying to produce a record. Carl Perkins was in the studio, playing guitar in several cuts. Every few minutes a large, barefoot, suet-thighed lady turned to Huey Meaux and yelled, "Make Carl Perkins play the 'Blue Suede Shoes'! Please!" Carl, a reformed alky, seemed ill at ease.

Billy Lee Riley, the man who cut "Flying Saucers Rock 'n' Roll" for Sun in 1957, materialized, looking like 5,000 concentrated volts. He spread his hands before him as if holding a birthday cake. "Man, I got me a pill this big, and when I take a bite the damn thing grows right back." Then he smiled, baring a large space between his teeth, and departed quickly.

It was the only recording session I ever saw that was fun.

In a Fort Lauderdale club in the spring of 1973, my friend Al Bianculli taped several hours of Jerry Lee speaking. Judd and Pappy were there, but mostly unconscious.

"Jerry, what were you doing between 1952 and 1956?"

"I don't remember. I was a ramblin' man, a gamblin' man. . . . My ancestors come from Alabama. Come by covered wagon. Settled in Lewiston, Louisiana. . . . Still own the town, the Lewises. . . . They did, they settled there, in Lewiston. . . . They own that town. Lewiston,

Louisiana. Nice town. They sent me a telegram when I done the Steve Allen show, complimenting me, you know. . . . 'We'd love to meet you sometime.' Said who they were. And, hell, they're worth millions, as far as money goes. They wouldn't tolerate daddy or [unintelligible] or [unintelligible]. . . . My great-grandfather owned a plantation. He owned Monroe, Louisiana. *Owned* it, lock, stock, and barrel. That's Louisiana history. Old Man Lewis. He had a hundred and fifty slaves. Then they freed all the slaves. He wasn't a slavedriver or anything. They made 'em leave. . . . He owned it. . . . I can show you the house where he was raised up himself, the house that he owned. . . . That big funeral home right there on Ouichita Cliff, right in Monroe, Louisiana. That was his home. . . . Monroe was once all a plantation. If you think I'm tellin' you a lie, you just check your history book. It's taught in history books. . . . J. P. Hardy's Little Club, the one I worked in . . . [unintelligible] . . . called it the Little Club. . . . I worked out there way over on—what's that street? That big old place out there. I was 18 years old. I played out there, and this guy was crippled. He's crippled. Had hands like this. Played his guitar like this. And he can *play*. He was workin' out there, and had this guy on steel guitar, one of the greatest steel guitar-players you ever heard in your life. . . . And that's the first time I met Otis Brown. He walked in, and at that time he was a hell of a man; he had them sleeves rolled up. And, boy, you could tell that he was a tough shot. So he wiped out about six. Had a few beers. And then he wanted to come up and play fiddle. And I thought he could play! And he was Aunt Jane's son. I never met [unintelligible], didn't know him, period. But Otis Brown I knew, I'd heard of him. I thought he could play. He got up there and—he, you know, he was my first cousin—so the steel guitar-player says, 'That sonofabitch can't play nothin'.' Made me mad, y'know? And he was right, he couldn't [laughs]. . . . Well, son, I've lived a hell of a life. You wouldn't believe the experiences. . . . How many things are there left for me to do? How many roads am I to travel? Or am I livin' in my final hour? . . . [fades]. . . .

"Jim Reeves. He's a good old boy, but you haveta get to know him. [Reeves died in a plane crash in 1964.] A strange person. We had some

Jerry Lee Lewis and his cousin Mickey Gilley, 1976.

pretty good times together. Yeah, he drank. At that time I didn't drink that much. He did. He did drink pretty good, I know that, he drank pretty good. He told me, 'I'll tell ya, if RCA ever brings me out to do another record hop without the right kind of band, they can kiss my ass.' That's the first time I'd ever met him. I said, 'What's your problem?' He said, 'I just don't like that band.' And the guy that's playin' drums is just beatin' on it: boom-a-boom-boom-a. You wouldn't believe it. Jim Reeves went out there with his guitar and he said, 'Boys'—and he was real nice; I knew right then, there's a pro—he says, 'I don't think I need ya to back me up. Just lay out and let me play the guitar.' Just him and the guitar, and it was beautiful. He hung it in. He tore 'em up, man. He proved his point. And I come, 'Great Balls of Fire,' and that damn band. Cat out there with a moustache had a bass drum hung round his neck and he's beatin' on it. . . . Me and Jim got together after that and we made every club in town. . . . He was a fine person. . . . Strange cat, just couldn't get close to him. . . . He did 'Four Walls.' Just him and a guitar. He liked me, though. He enjoyed gettin' with me, and he'd drink. . . . Jim Reeves, Merle Haggard, they're two funny cats. Great talents, but funny cats. . . . Hell, I don't care about it myself. I'll fight my way through those damn hotels and I'll be nice and I'll be a piano-player and I'll sing and I'll just be what I am. I ain't gonna be no strange cat. I ain't gonna back off in no corner and hide. . . . You're gettin' a hell of an interview, ain't ya? . . . [fades]. . . .

"Dr. Jekyll and Mr. Hyde. That's what that bitch always called me. . . . The Killer! . . . [Pappy wakens, yells: 'Killer Diller!']. . . . Armadilla! . . . Know what armadillas are?"

"Amarillo, Texas?"

"Hell, Louisiana's got more of 'em than Texas. Grave robbers, them things."

"Is that how you got the name 'Killer'?"

"WHAT!"

"You said, 'Killer Diller,' and then you said, 'Amarillo!' "

"Arro-dillo! You know what arro-*dillos* are?"

"I never seen one in person, but I seen pictures of 'em."

"Then you know what I'm talkin' about, doncha? That ain't where I got the name 'Killer.' I ain't a grave robber. You callin' me a grave robber? What the fuck are you talkin' about! Damn . . ."

Patsy Lynn Kochin, esteemed deposed president of the Jerry Lee Lewis Fan Club, told in her *Newsletter* of a night she spent with Jerry Lee in a Boston Ramada Inn. It is one of my favorite passages.

"Jerry would play the piano with one hand and sing while he found what he was looking for in the Bible using the other hand. He then read Acts Ch. 2. . . . Jerry also spoke on the last days which he says we are

Jerry Lee Lewis confronts the light of Horus.
Photo by Charlyn Zlotnik.

Think about it.

living in—the end almost here. . . . Then he told us why the South lost the war. . . . Jerry then explained the difference in a 99 year sentence and a 100 year sentence. . . ."

The truth is that Jerry Lee has always known the end is almost here, must be almost here, and that the almost-here end is the heart of it all; without it, there is no rock-and-roll, no jukebox epiphany, just pale, soft people looking from the window. Without the obsession or the fever or the fear of the almost-here end, all is reasonable and mere.

Somehow that is why Jerry Lee Lewis leaned with a loaded gun beneath the window of Elvis Presley in the hour of the wolf. Elvis had turned his back on the Church of the Almost-Here End, sold his soul to MOR, but Jerry Lee kept pumping—Holiness! Tongues!—and with each new clawsome, wild wife, with every new midnight violence, every extravagance of face, he slid further from grace. The King and the Killer: this was their desert. To Elvis it was a droll annoyance, but to Jerry Lee the midnight deed was glory, no mere D&D scene, but 1 Sam. 17:49, .38-style. In the cold, brilliant handcuffs the creature known in certain parts of Mississippi as Colonel Hermes Trismegistus, in parts of Tennessee as God's Garbage Man, squinted into the dark and thought a thought: Did they have Breathalizers in the Old Testament days?

On May 3, 1977, Memphis City Court Judge Albert Boyd declared Jerry Lee Lewis not guilty of the charges for which he was arrested at 3764 Elvis Presley Boulevard the previous November. Rock on, Judge.

May the voice never end that for so long has said these words of virtue: "Just gimme my money and show me where the piano is." If it does, so does the Church.

Jerry Lee's 1958 scandal marked the beginning of the end for Sun. In 1957 Jerry Lee, Johnny Cash, and Bill Justis had given Sam Phillips great crossover hits. By the fall of 1958 Lewis and Justis had ceased to have hits, and Cash had signed with Columbia. Judd Phillips went up against payola allegations, and he and Sam broke their relationship.

"I think Sam's problem," said Judd in 1972, "was that he never really believed in them—he was afraid. He never really had faith. He

WELCOME DEEJAYS

And

THANK YOU

For

Your Wonderful Help

JOHNNY CASH

———

Star of   **WSM—Grand**

Sun Records   **Ole Opry**

THANKS

Friends Everywhere

For Liking My

"Home Of The Blues"

"Give My Love To Rose"

———

Exclusive Management:

BOB NEAL

1916 Sterick Bldg.

Memphis, Tennessee

never really believed that Elvis Presley, Jerry Lee Lewis, Johnny Cash would be the giants they are today. He thought it was just a passing situation. And as a consequence we let all these artists slip away from us."

In the summer of 1958 Judd formed his own company, Judd Records, in Sheffield, Alabama. (In 1960 he sold out to NRC in Atlanta.) Early in 1959 producer Jack Clement, who had been at Sun since 1955 and had been responsible for much of Sun's most imaginative production work (such as Jerry Lee's 1957 doo-wop recording of Hank Williams's "You Win Again"), was fired by Sam after a disagreement.

*An early Judd record, by former Sun guitarist Roland Janes
(his name was misspelled on the label).*

Early in 1961 Sam opened a studio at 17th Avenue in Nashville. He began using many of the city's pop-country musicians in his sessions: Floyd Cramer, Hank Garland, Buddy Harmon, Bob Moore, Pig Robbins, Billy Sherrill, and others. But Phillips failed to make Sun a part of the ever more lucrative Nashville sound.

Sun lingered. In 1966 Sam shut Phillips International, the subsidiary he had formed in the fall of 1957. From 1964 to 1968, Sun released only 20 singles, most of them junk. In 1968 Sun Records came to its end. On July 1, 1969, Nashville entrepreneur Shelby Singleton, Jr., acquired from Sam 80 percent interest in the Sun catalogue and became the major stockholder in a new Sun International Corporation. Since 1969 Singleton has released a flow of budget-line Sun reissues.

A record on Sam Phillips's short-lived Holiday Inn label, 1968.

Presley, Perkins, and Lewis were the most famous, most successful rockabilly artists. Others, less enduring, less famed, made music often as good, sometimes better.

Vincent Gene Craddock, better known as Gene Vincent, was born in Norfolk, Virginia, on February 11, 1935. He served in the navy during the Korean War and was severely hurt in combat. Doctors thought that his leg must be amputated, but Vincent did not allow the operation and instead wore a leg brace through the rest of his life. Thin, wan, crippled, Vincent was an unlikely pop star, but a pop star he nonetheless became.

After performing at station WCMS, Vincent and his band, the Blue Caps, were brought to Capitol by Sheriff Tex Davis, who worked at WCMS. In the spring of 1956 his first disk was released: "Be-Bop-A-Lula" (inspired by a *Little Lulu* comic) c / w "Woman Love." On the country charts "Be-Bop-A-Lula" hit Number Five, and on the pop charts Number Nine. Basically a light, cute lyric, until Vincent delivered it with psychopathy. It was a perverse, gothic performance, and one of the perfect rockabilly performances. "Woman Love" was an obvious emulation of Elvis, but it possessed the powerful sense of the macabre that came to be Vincent's trademark. It is an overtly sexual record, full of glottal twitches and orgasmic pantings.

"Be-Bop-A-Lula" was Vincent's only country hit, and his only Top Ten pop hit. Capitol issued 19 singles by Vincent before he left the label in 1961. During the next 10 years, he recorded for Challenge, Forever, Dandelion, and Kama Sutra, all without commercial success. On October 12, 1971, Gene Vincent died in Saugus, California, from internal hemorrhaging. He was 36 and drunk.

Of the major rockabilly artists, Buddy Holly alone never had a hit record on the country charts. Born Charles Hardin Holly in Lubbock, Texas, on September 7, 1936, Buddy's musical heritage was hard-core country, but by the mid fifties he had developed an interest in black music. After several years of clubs and radio in the Lubbock area, Holly was signed to Decca early in 1956, and on January 26, in Nashville, Owen Bradley produced Holly's first session. In April a single was released: "Blue Days, Black Nights" and "Love Me." Four more disks followed, including the classic "That'll Be the Day," but little happened. In March 1957, Buddy Holly and the Crickets were signed to

Brunswick / Coral, and late that year "Peggy Sue" became Holly's first hit, eventually rising to Number Three on the pop charts. Within the next two years, Holly had five more pop hits, but none entered the Top Ten.

On February 3, 1959, near Fargo, North Dakota, an airplane carrying Holly, Richie Valens, and the Big Bopper (J. P. Richardson) crashed, killing all aboard. Waylon Jennings, who was in Holly's band at the time, gave his seat to the Big Bopper at the last minute.

Although Buddy Holly was a rockabilly artist, he was very different from the rockabilly mainstream. His was a softer music, and his records sounded less neurotic, effervescent instead of turbulent. All was tasteful, nothing clashed. Holly was the gentleman of rockabilly, the first soft rocker. In Holly's records, rockabilly deflects from country music toward a more refined, Apollonian form, perhaps best exemplified by the music of the Everly Brothers, who thrived from 1957 to 1961. With their harmonious sound and rosy-romantic material, the Everly Brothers were the pivotal rockabilly act, rooted deeper in pop than in country. This was the last, inevitable current. With Buddy Holly the mania had ebbed. Now it was nothing but a genetic echo.

In 1957 pop singer Guy Mitchell recorded "Rock-a-Billy" for Columbia, and it hit the Top Twenty. By October there was a 20th Century–Fox film *Rockabilly Baby,* starring Les Brown and Irene Ryan. It was over.

The country-music corpus reacted in its way to rockabilly. Johnny Cash, who was not really a rockabilly artist, was the butt of bigotry in Nashville simply because he recorded for Sun (1955–1958). In 1976 Cash said, "Y'know, myself, back in '56, I had a hard time breaking into the country-music community in Nashville. I came up to the Grand Ole Opry to talk to Jim Denny, who was the manager of the Opry. 'I Walk the Line' was Number One. I had an appointment—but I sat in his outer office about two hours before he ever saw me. Finally he let me come in, and the very first question was, 'What makes you think you belong on the Grand Ole Opry?' "

In 1974 Faron Young spoke of rockabilly: "I said, yeah, Jerry, I remember when you were cutting 'Whole Lotta Shakin' '—you didn't give a damn whether country music existed or not. You better get down on your knees every night and thank the Lord for Webb Pierce and Faron Young and Hank Snow—that they kept working and kept this business alive so you'd have something to come back to. If it had been left up to you back then, you wouldn't have given a damn if it had gone plumb under.''

Many old-line country artists tried to cash in on rockabilly. Good taste is timeless, but money is better. The month after Elvis's first record was released, RCA-Victor issued "Hep Cat Baby" by Eddy Arnold (the song was written by Tin Pan Alley veteran Cy Coben); it hit Number Nine on the country charts. Bill Monroe went and cut a new version of "Blue Moon of Kentucky" later in the year, and Marty Robbins, who had joined the Opry in 1953, covered "That's All Right" for Columbia (it rose to Number Nine). In 1955 Billy Jack Wills (Bob Wills's youngest brother) cut "There's Good Rockin' Tonight" for MGM.

In 1956 came "Country Boy Rock 'n' Roll" by Don Reno & Red Smiley (King), "Hula Rock" by Hank Snow (RCA-Victor), "So Let's Rock" by Bob Wills (Decca), and "Teen-Age Boogie" by Webb Pierce (Decca). In 1957 came "Rock & Roll Fever" by Cecil Campbell (MGM), "Rockin' and Rollin' " by Carson Robison (MGM; Robison always rolled with the current—at the height of the McCarthy hearings, he had recorded "I'm No Communist"), and "Shake Baby Shake" by Wayne Raney (Decca). In 1958 came Tex Williams's belated exhortation to "Let's Go Rockabilly" (Decca).

A few country artists were stimulated in a good way by rockabilly. Arthur Smith's 1958 "Guitar Bustin' " (MGM) is a killer, and Little Jimmy Dickens's 1958 "I Got a Hole in My Pocket" (Columbia) created a roaring hard-rock sound that foreshadowed things to come.

There were also closet rockabilly singers. George Jones cut "Rock It" and "Heartbreak Hotel" for Starday under the name of Thumper Jones. (His "Heartbreak Hotel" was also issued by Tops under the name of Hank Smith and the Nashville Playboys). Cowboy Copas used his real name, Lloyd Copas, when he cut "Circle Rock" for Decca. Johnny Dee, who recorded rock songs such as "Sittin' in the Balcony" and "Teenage Queen" for Colonial, a Chapel Hill, North Carolina, label, was really John D. Loudermilk. Some of Buck Owens's 1957 rockabilly records, cut for Pep and Chesterfield, listed the singer's name as Corky Jones. Johnny Paycheck had not yet changed his name from Donny Young when he recorded "Shaking the Blues" and other rockers for Decca in 1960. (Paycheck's real name is David Lytle. He got his current name from Johnny Paychek, a small-time heavyweight who was KO'd by Joe Louis in two rounds in 1940.)

When I asked George Jones about his Thumper Jones recordings, he said, "I don't guess I'm gonna ever live that down. I was actually getting started in the business about 1954 or so when all this rock-and-roll really started movin' in, and of course, you know, you didn't have stations back then that played all that much country to start with. So especially with rock-and-roll getting as strong as it was at that time, it seemed like country music was really a losin' battle except for the three or four major artists that had it made at the time, like Lefty Frizzell, Ernest Tubb, Roy Acuff, some of those people. So we decided to try one, sorta rockabilly like. I was sorta ashamed to even do it at the time 'cause I was so country, so I just used a different name, went under the name of Thumper Jones."

George did like Elvis, however. "Oh, yes, quite a bit. I liked quite a bit of the things that came out then, because really you didn't have much else to like. You didn't have the radio stations playin' enough of the country music for you to really have a chance to listen to nothin' but country, so it was a lot of it forced upon us really."

Even Northern R&B labels tried to stick their hands up rockabilly's skirt. In 1956 Fortune Records of Detroit released "You Ain't No Good for Me" by Elvis imitator Jimmy Lee. United Records of Chicago released a rockabilly "Honey Hush" by John Hampton in 1957. The next year, Apollo in New York issued "You Shake Me Up" by Andy Anderson, and Federal in Cincinnati released "Mercy, Mercy, Mercy" by Joe Penny. Rockabilly records by black artists, such as G. L. Crockett's 1957 "Look Out Mabel" on Chief, a Chicago blues label, were rare.

Rockabilly left a deep mark on both country music and rock. When the Beatles reached America in 1964, they came with a version of Carl

George Jones, c. 1945.

George Jones, c. 1965.

Perkins's "Matchbox" that glimmered like holy water. In country music, traces of rockabilly run thick. Hear Mickey Gilley (Jerry Lee's cousin), or Gary Stewart, or a hundred other men.

Billy Swan, born May 12, 1942, in Cape Girardeau, Missouri, is a Nashville songwriter and singer who cut his teeth on rockabilly. (His home town is on the Mississippi, about 200 miles above Memphis.) While attending high school, Swan wrote Clyde McPhatter's 1962 hit "Lover Please." In Nashville he joined with Kris Kristofferson, the man who changed the chemistry of country-music songwriting. (The

94

emotional heat and literacy of Kris's songs were so unfamiliar to Nashville in the late sixties that some of his best work, such as "Help Me Make It Through the Night" and "Me and Bobby McGee," was turned down by numerous singers.) Swan cut a handful of singles for MGM, Rising Sons, and Monument. Then in 1974 he shocked the music industry with "I Can Help," a cool, raunchy rockabilly record that grew into one of the year's biggest international hits.

A different kind of modern rockabilly is that of Delbert McClinton. Born in Lubbock, Texas, on November 4, 1940, and raised in Fort Worth, Delbert cut his first record in 1959, "Wake Up Baby" (a Sonny Boy Williamson song) for Major Bill Smith's LeCam label. (At the request of Major Bill, who is sort of a bargain-basement Colonel Parker, Delbert's name was altered to Mac Clinton.) In 1962 he played harmonica in "Hey! Baby," the 1962 Smash hit by Bruce Channel, a country singer from Grapevine, Texas, who indulged in the pop sounds of the early sixties. When Bruce and Delbert toured England after "Hey! Baby," the Beatles were the opening act for them at the Castle in New Brighton. The boys from across the Mersey had never heard a harmonica played as Delbert played it, and they kept after him to teach them licks. A few months later, in December 1962, the Beatles had their first hit, "Love Me Do," the distillation of the rock-and-roll harmonica lessons learned from Delbert. Today Bruce Channel works for the Parks Department in Grapevine. In the mid sixties Delbert recorded with the Rondells, a Fort Worth group, for labels such as LeCam, Shalimar, and Smash; as Del McClinton, he cut some singles for London. In 1972 and 1973 he and his friend Glen Clark recorded two albums for Clean, a short-lived subsidiary of Atlantic, under the name Delbert & Glen: *Delbert & Glen* and *Subject to Change.* In 1975 Delbert signed with ABC, and in three beautiful albums *(Victim of Life's Circumstances, Genuine Cowhide,* and *Love Rustler)* he wrought a mixture of Southern R&B, honky-tonk, and his own awesome writing skills.

McClinton is one of the few people who write perfect songs, seething with concise rhythm and bare of useless words—Pindar with a rock pulse.

Rock was feared and hated by so many. Some reacted in an almost medieval manner. In August 1955, Rev. Robert Gray of Trinity Baptist Church in Jacksonville, Florida, yelled to his congregation that Elvis Presley had "achieved a new low in spiritual degeneracy."

In 1956 Billy Rose spoke before the Anti-Trust Subcommittee of the House Judiciary Committee. (In 1953, the year of Bill Haley's "Crazy, Man, Crazy," the Songwriters of America had filed an antitrust action against BMI, accusing that company of conspiracy "to dominate and control the market for the use and exploitation of musical compositions.") Said Billy Rose, "Not only are most of the BMI songs junk, but in many cases they are obscene junk. . . . It is the current climate on radio and TV which makes Elvis Presley and his animal posturings possible." Mr. Rose's compositions include "Barney Google," "You Tell Her I Stutter," and "I Got a Code id by Dose."

At a press conference in Washington, D.C., in 1957, actress Helen Hayes claimed that her son (later known as James MacArthur, sidekick of Jack Lord in *Hawaii Five-O*) had been well on the path to juvenile delinquency, brought on by rock-and-roll records. She cured him by playing a Beethoven record.

Same year, same place: Vance Packard, author of *The Hidden Persuaders,* said, "Our airways have been flooded in recent years with whining guitarists, musical riots put to switchblade beat, obscure lyrics about hugging, squeezing, and rocking all night long."

In October 1976, Darryl Faulk, youth pastor of the Capitol Assembly of God Church in Carson City, Nevada, rose to cry that "most Christians are not aware that secular music is poison." From somewhere the pastor recruited 20 young people to make a public pyre of rock-and-roll albums. The fire department, however, stopped this exhibition, saying that when consumed by fire, polyvinyl gives off toxic fumes. The pastor and his army compromised: They burned the album jackets and stomped hell out of the records. This was said to have had a more droll, less evangelical effect than intended.

Emmett Miller, 1

Emmett Miller is one of the most intriguing and profoundly important men in the history of country music.

He was the first recording artist to sing in the wry, bluesy yodeling style that was later associated with Jimmie Rodgers. He was also the first country singer to record with horns and drums. The mongrel jazz-country music of Bob Wills is rooted strongly in the work of Emmett Miller. In his September 23, 1935, recording of "I Ain't Got Nobody," issued on the Vocalion label, Wills plainly imitated Miller's earlier recording of the song. Wills even patterned much of his persona and many of his mannerisms on those of Miller, most notably the jivey exclamations and detached comments that interpolate most of his recordings. (It is laughable that in his otherwise impressive biography of Wills, *San Antonio Rose,* Charles R. Townsend devotes only four thin sentences to Miller's influence on Wills. Dr. Townsend prefers to believe that Wills's musical mannerisms derived from his moiling in the cotton fields, shoulder-to-shoulder with black sharecroppers, but the truth of the matter is that young Bob Wills was what might be described as a well-to-do white kid. In 1919, when Bob was fourteen years old, his father had an income in excess of $20,000. In 1919, mind you.)

It is not known exactly when Emmett Miller was born or when he died. Nor is it known where he came from or where he went. We don't even know what he looked like, really.

Emmett Miller was a white man from the South, born late in the nineteenth century. On October 25, 1924, he made his first record,

"Anytime," for Okeh in New York City. On November 7, 1924, Miller had his second Okeh session in New York City, and the result was "The Pickaninnies' Paradise." I've never heard either of these records, nor do I know of anyone who has.

Miller's third Okeh session was on September 1, 1925, in Asheville, North Carolina. Four records resulted: "Big Bad Bill Is Sweet William Now" c / w "Lovesick Blues"; "You're Just the Girl for Me" c / w "I Never Had the Blues"; "Brother Bill" c / w "Thousand Frogs"; and "Hungry Sam" c / w "Sam and His Family." Piano, drums, and horns were used. The last four sides are funny black-dialect routines with jazzy musical backdrops; an unknown man performs as straight-man to Miller in these records. More than any of his other work, these rare performances give credence to the theory that Miller worked as a blackface comedian.

He did not record again until June 12, 1928, when he cut four sides at the Okeh studio in New York: "God's River Blues," "I Ain't Got Nobody," a new version of "Lovesick Blues," and "Lion Tamers." The musicians in this session were Tommy Dorsey (trombone), Jimmy Dorsey (clarinet and alto sax), Eddie Lang (guitar), Leo McConville (trumpet), Stan King (drums), and Arthur Schutt (piano). A man named Dan Fitch assisted Miller in the brief dialogues that prefaced many of the cuts. These records were issued under the name of Emmett Miller and His Georgia Crackers, as were his later Okeh releases.

Miller had six more Okeh sessions in New York. With slight variations, the same Georgia Crackers were used.

August 9, 1928 (Manny Klein may have replaced Leo McConville on trumpet): "Anytime" and "St. Louis Blues."

September 14, 1928: "Take Your Tomorrow" and "Dusky Stevedore."

January 8, 1929 (the voice of Charles Chiles was added in the last song): "I Ain't Gonna Give Nobody None of My Jelly-Roll," "She's Funny That Way," and "You Lose."

January 19, 1929 (Joe Tarto was added on bass): "Right or Wrong," "That's the Good Old Sunny South," and "You're the Cream in My Coffee."

September 5, 1929 (Leo McConville may have replaced Manny Klein on trumpet, and the voice of Phil Pavey, who had cut two records for Okeh in February, was added in the last song): "Lovin' Sam," "Big Bad Bill Is Sweet William Now," and "The Ghost of the St. Louis Blues."

September 12, 1929 (Gene Krupa replaced Stan King on drums): "Sweet Mama (Papa's Getting Mad)," "The Pickaninnies' Paradise," and "The Blues Singer from Alabam'."

Several of these recordings were issued in England on the Parlophone label, and in France and Germany on the Odeon label.

In Atlanta on September 24 and 25, 1929, Miller joined Fiddlin' John Carson, Frank Hutchison, Narmour and Smith, Moonshine Kate, Bud Blue, the Black Brothers, and Martin Malloy to record "The Medicine Show," a three-disk revue of music and comedy.

On September 1, 1936, Miller emerged in New York to cut four sides for Bluebird. The personnel are unknown, except that Gene Cobb sang in the first three cuts. These were Miller's final recordings: "I Ain't Got Nobody," "The Gypsy," "Anytime," and "Right or Wrong."

Then Emmett Miller vanished.

Most of those who knew Miller are dead. In 1976 I called Joe Tarto, who had played bass in Miller's last three New York Okeh sessions. Tarto now lives in New Jersey.

"The only Miller that I knew was Eddie Miller," said Joe Tarto.

"But you played in three of Emmett Miller's sessions, didn't you?"

"Glenn Miller?"

"No. *Emmett* Miller. You played on his records."

"To be honest with you, I don't recall. There was so many of them I lost track. I really did."

Joe Tarto suggested I call Chauncey Morehouse, a popular jazz drummer of the 1920s and '30s who Tarto said had a good memory. Morehouse also lives in New Jersey. While he was able to give me some interesting information on the lesser-known musicians in Miller's records (Chauncey recalled that Stan King was well known for his unswayable beat, that Arthur Schutt was an awesomely heavy drinker, and that Manny Klein, a houseman in the NBC band with Chauncey, once played with Toscanini), he had no memory of Emmett Miller.

"The only Emmett I ever knew was back in Chambersburg, Pennsylvania. Emmett Waugaman. His father ran a drugstore."

"And Emmett Kelly, the clown," added Mrs. Morehouse, who was listening on another line.

"When we were at NBC," said Chauncey, "the dates came so fast that we'd go out and do a date and come home and I'd be layin' in bed at night and I'd think, 'Who in the hell was the leader of that session?' We were always working. It's hard to remember. A lot of guys thought Chauncey was a fag name."

Finally I was led to Seger Ellis, a jazz pianist, who recalls meeting Emmett Miller at the Okeh studio in the Amalgamated Bank Building at Union Square in Manhattan. Ellis, who was born in 1904, has lived in Houston for many years.

"I was under contract to Okeh at the time he recorded. [Ellis recorded for Okeh from November 30, 1926, to November 23, 1930. In the late 1940s, Ellis cut some country-pop sides for Victor under the name of Harry Houston, a name suggested by Steve Sholes. He says he enjoyed listening to country music when he was younger.] He used to do a lot of yodeling, right? He was probably in his late twenties or maybe early thirties then. I think he was about a medium-sized man, a little on the plump side, if I remember correctly. I think he was balding. He'd lost most of his hair, or a lot of it. And he was definitely from the South, either Texas or Arkansas, I believe. I'm not sure. I only met him the one time. He had a big seller. I can't remember the name of it. He was no kid at the time; he'd been battling around for a long time. He happened to make this one record for Okeh and it sold real big and they got him back for another one, and the next session he didn't have anything that moved at all. And that was sort of the end of him. I think he played some guitar, but not on record.

"He was a fun-loving guy, it seems. He was also sort of a loner, as far as I know. I don't know anybody who knew him real well. They didn't even know him real well around Okeh, I don't believe."

Ellis, who had used the Dorseys in many of his sessions, assured me that Emmett Miller's music "wasn't the kind of stuff they wanted to play. It was just a record date to them. It would've been Justin Ring's idea. He was musical director down at Okeh, and he practically A&R'd everybody's dates. He's dead now."

I asked Seger if Miller was considered a jazz singer or a country singer. "Oh, definitely country."

The mystery of Emmett Miller, I think, will never be penetrated. Perhaps someday a trunk of Miller lore will be discovered in the basement of a long-shuttered Hattiesburg whorehouse. Perhaps someday, some further day, Miller will be revealed to have been a truant Tau Ceti cartographer. Perhaps he operates a candy store in Bayonne.

The surviving Emmett Miller disks are among the rarest of records. Several years ago, a West Coast bootleg label called the Old Masters inaugurated a series of jazz reissue albums with *Emmet Miller Acc. by His Georgia Crackers,* a set of 14 Okeh sides. There were no liner notes or illustrations, and Emmett's name was misspelled. But the music was there, pressed in beautiful clear green plastic. Now that album, released in an edition of 1000, is itself a rarity.

The unavailability of Emmett Miller's recordings is mournable, for his music is as striking and bizarre in these days as it was in the 1920s. When I played Miller's version of "Lovesick Blues" for Peter Stampfel, his jaw dropped in ecstatic reflex. There was never another voice like Miller's. Seger Ellis called it "freakish"; it was congested, nasal, full of after-hours liquor and crazy times. He often swirled his lyrics off into high, weird yodels—a manic but wholly pleasant effect. He was the greatest song stylist of his generation, and until Jerry Lee Lewis came along no one jumped songs with such sheer redneck class.

Yodeling Cowboys and Such

The word *yodel* is from the German *jodeln,* which means, literally, to utter the sound *jo.*

In the early nineteenth century, performances of yodelers were common on the British stage. Sir Walter Scott in his *Journal* entry of June 4, 1830, wrote that, "Anne wants me to go to hear the Tyrolese Minstrels, but . . . I cannot but think their yodeling . . . is a variation upon the tones of a jackass."

Yodeling became a part of American minstrelsy. The first yodeling minstrel was Tom Christian, who made his debut in Chicago in 1847. Daniel Decatur Emmett (1815–1904), the composer and minstrel who wrote "Dixie" in 1859 for Bryant's Minstrels, was the author of several songs that showcased what he had learned from visiting European showmen.

The first yodeler to make records was George P. Watson, who cut several cylinders for the Edison company. His earliest were *"Leben auf den Alpen"* and "Emmett's German Yodle," both released in 1897. Watson recorded three more of Dan Emmett's compositions: "Emmett's Lullaby," released in 1899, and "Medley of Emmett's Yodles" and "Emmett's Yodle Song," both released in 1901.

Yodel records were most popular during the first two decades of the twentieth century. A Columbia catalogue of 1917 includes a section, with many selections by George Watson. A 1920 Victor catalogue lists seventeen Yodel Songs, and again many of them are by George Watson (recording contracts were not what they are today).

The first country record to include yodeling was "Rock All Our

Babies to Sleep," cut by the blind Georgia singer Riley Puckett (1894–1946) for Columbia in April 1924. The following September, Puckett recorded his second yodel disk, "Sleep, Baby, Sleep." George Watson had recorded English and German versions of this song for Edison in 1897. (The song itself was an 1869 hit by S. A. Emery.) At his first recording session on August 4, 1927, in Bristol, Tennessee, Jimmie Rodgers also cut "Sleep, Baby, Sleep," the first yodel record by the man who became famous as America's Blue Yodeler.

A Jimmie Rodgers endorsement of Weymann guitars, in the April 1930 issue of The Metronome.

Herb Quinn, a black musician who lived near Rodgers in Mississippi in the early twenties, says that Rodgers's blue yodeling was much copied by both white and black musicians of the era. In Quinn's phrase, "everyone who could pick a guitar" started yodeling like Rodgers.

THE WORLD'S GREATEST BLUES SINGER

BESSIE SMITH
WITH HER ALL-STAR REVUE
SPECIAL SHOW FOR WHITE PEOPLE
BIJOU Theater--TONIGHT 10:45
REGULAR SHOW 8:30—COLORED ONLY
"PASSED BY THE BOARD OF CENSORSHIP"
PHONE 6-5981 FOR SEATS

A Complete Stock of

BESSIE SMITH
COLUMBIA RECORDS
—ON SALE AT—

Phone
6-9158
B-O-N-D-S
38
Arcade
GRAPHOPHONE SHOP

Advertisement, Nashville Banner, November 30, 1926.

A few blues singers yodeled on record, such as Tampa Red in "Worried Devil Blues" (Bluebird, 1934). Bessie Smith had cut "Yodeling Blues" for Columbia in 1923, but she didn't bother to yodel. Perhaps Bessie yodeled when she performed the song in concert; if she did, it's likely that Jimmie Rodgers heard her.

Rodgers was the most famous of country music's blue yodelers, and several important singers copied his style directly. The best-known Rodgers imitators are Jimmie Davis and Gene Autry, who both started recording in 1929.

I think the mysterious Emmett Miller blue-yodeled earlier and better

*Mrs. Jimmie Rodgers's threnody for her husband,
"played on Jimmie Rodgers' own guitar."*

*A 1933 advertisement for Gene Autry's record "The Death of Jimmie Rodgers." Autry
and Art Satherly of ARC conceived and scheduled the recording before Rodgers died.*

Ernest Tubb's first record, "The Last Thoughts of Jimmie Rodgers," written by Rodgers's sister-in-law Elsie McWilliams and cut by Tubb for Victor in October 1936, was recorded again in 1953 for this tribute EP.

than Jimmie Rodgers. One of the best-known yodeling performances in country music, Hank Williams's "Lovesick Blues," would not have been without Miller.

"Lovesick Blues" was copyrighted on April 3, 1922, by Jack Mills, Inc., in New York City. The words were written by Irving Mills (born on January 16, 1894, in Russia; Mills later wrote many more standards, such as "It Don't Mean a Thing If It Ain't Got That Swing," "Mood Indigo," and "Caravan"); the music was written by vaudeville piano-player Cliff Friend (born on October 1, 1893, in Cincinnati). Later, Cliff Friend held that he sold all his rights to "Lovesick Blues" for $500.

Emmett Miller recorded his first version of the song, with yodeling, on September 1, 1925, in Asheville, North Carolina, and it was released by Okeh during the next month. In 1927 blues singer Bertha Chippie Hill also recorded the song for Okeh. On June 12, 1928, Miller cut another version of "Lovesick Blues" in New York City, this time with several well-known jazz musicians behind him (Tommy Dorsey, Jimmy Dorsey, Eddie Lang, and others). Again Miller yodeled. The record was released by Okeh in July 1928, c/w "Big Bad Bill Is Sweet William Now." The disk bore the name of Emmett Miller and His Georgia Crackers.

In December 1939, Rex Griffin, the Alabama-born honky-tonk singer who had written the classic suicide song, "The Last Letter," in 1937, released "Lovesick Blues" on Decca. Griffin's version is a paragon of simplicity: The only accompaniment is his own acoustic guitar. Vocally, Griffin copied Miller in every accessible way, including the wholly strange yodeling that was Miller's watermark. As similar to Miller's version as it is, Rex Griffin's "Lovesick Blues" is a hillbilly song, pure and simple.

Hank Williams copied "Lovesick Blues" directly from Rex Griffin's record. He began singing it at the Louisiana Hayride early in 1949 and recorded it for MGM soon after. When he performed it during his debut at the Grand Ole Opry on June 11, 1949, he became myth, the archetypal country singer. Released on February 25, 1949, Hank's "Lovesick Blues" stayed on the charts for 42 weeks, the most successful country record of the year. To many people the song, like Hank, is archetypally country. There are those who would not hear that it was written by a Jew from Russia, that it was midwived by a redneck jazz singer who would have been puked off the Opry.

Many different styles of yodeling could be heard in country records of the 1920s and early '30s: the archaic, nineteenth-century yodel, which can be heard in records such as "Rockin' Yodel" by the Leake County Revelers (Columbia, 1928) and "We Have Moonshine in the West Virginia Hills" by Harvey and Earl Shirky (Columbia, 1930); the minstrel-show yodel, a sort of fake blue yodel (Swiss yodel, black lyrics) that probably predated the yodeling of both Rodgers and Miller, heard in records such as Frank Welling's "Yodelin' Daddy Blues" (Super-tone, 1929); and pop-country yodeling, as in Jimmy Long's "Yodel Your Troubles Away" (Champion, 1929).

For me, the ultimate country yodel record is the two-part "Yodel Blues" that Van and Pete recorded for Okeh in 1928. This is a great, dark, otherworldly piece of music that brings together the glimmering beads of a hundred ancient songs. There is a spare and brilliant steel guitar, hot and cold and monomaniacal, and a voice so seething with desolate power that it nearly chills the skin. The yodels here are not decorative, not, as Jimmie Rodgers called them, the "curlicues I can make with my throat," but feral and haunting, no closer to Switzerland than the nearest dark alley.

> *Well, I thought I heard*
> *A rumble down in the ground,*
> *Awooo, I said down in the ground;*
> *It was only the devil*
> *Chainin' his sweet mama down.*
> *There's a change in the ocean,*
> *In the deep blue sea:*
> *That sweet mama don't come back,*
> *You'll see a change in me.*

The novelty yodel reached an extreme in the early recording of Wilf Carter, or Montana Slim (born on December 18, 1904, in Guysboro,

Nova Scotia). Carter's Victor recordings featured what he called a three-in-one yodel, an effect that relied on the use of echo techniques in the studio.

After Jimmie Rodgers, many of the most successful country artists yodeled: Jimmie Davis, Gene Autry, Cliff Carlisle, and others. In the late 1930s, yodeling could even be heard in Western-swing records, such as "Blue Yodel #1" by Bob Wills and His Texas Playboys (1937) and "Dirty Hangover Blues" by W. Lee O'Daniel and His Hillbilly Boys (1939).

By the 1940s yodeling had become rare in country records. It seemed to represent an earlier, more boorish era, and singers and producers shook it loose. There were isolated, wonderful exceptions, such as Hank Williams's 1949 version of "Lovesick Blues."

Today very few country singers would dare yodel even if they could. Nevertheless, every Jerry Lee Lewis album includes at least one great, whiskey-drenched yodel. (Jerry Lee has been yodeling since the Sun days; he recorded "Lovesick Blues" in 1958 and Jimmie Rodgers's "Waiting for a Train" in 1962.) And Tompall Glaser yodeled in several recordings he made in 1975 and 1976, such as "T for Texas." Like Jerry Lee, Tompall is one of the very few singers who can interpret the classics of Rodgers and others in a knowing, exciting way.

In Hollywood in the 1930s was born the yodeling cowboy, one of the mightiest pop hallucinations of all time. Yodeling was not unknown among cowboys. By all accounts, it was no less common than fiddling among oceanographers or tromboning among rare book dealers.

Cowboys, real cowboys, did make records. One of the best cowboy singers was Jules Verne Allen (1883–1945), a cattle driver from Waxahachie, Texas, who worked in the last of the great drives from the Rio Grande to Montana. On April 21, 1928, in El Paso, Allen made his first sides for Victor. He cut six sessions, 24 songs in all, for Victor; the last was on April 27, 1929. Four of Allen's records were of noncowboy songs: "Po' Mourner," "Two Fragments," "You Mean Somebody But You Don't Mean Me," and "A Prisoner for Life" (the first two are of minstrelsy, the second pair pop). The remaining 20 records are all representative of cowboy music. "Zebra Dun" does not sound so unlike some of Hollywood's cowboy records (it is true that the early L.A. cowboy style was a mixture of the less esoteric cowboy songs and the singing styles of men such as Gene Autry), but some of Allen's other songs reveal a black influence that Hollywood ignored. (His "Jack o' Diamonds," for example, contains lyrics from "Make Me a Pallet on Your Floor.") Allen also cut a version of the classic "Chisolm Trail." The truth of "Chisolm Trail" is that it is a wondrously dirty song. It was recorded by folklorists in its original state (the Robert W. Gordon Collection of American Folk Song at the University of Oregon includes a dirty "Chisolm Trail," collected by Gordon in the late 1920s), but was rarely published. In his *Adventures of a Ballad Hunter* (1947), John A. Lomax wrote that some of the verses of "Chisolm Trail" would "burn up" the horn of the recording machine.

> *I fucked her standin' and I fucked her lyin',*
> *If she had wings I'd a-fucked her flyin'.*
> *The last time I seen her, and I ain't seen her since,*
> *She was scratchin' her cunt on a barb-wire fence.*

Included among the other authentic cowboy singers of the 1920s and early '30s were Dick Devall, J. D. Farley, Newton Gaines, Paul Hamblin, Billie Maxwell, Harry "Mac" McClinton, Carl T. Sprague, and Jack Webb. I think the ultimate cowboy record is "Texas Ranger," recorded by Jack and Bernard Cartwright for Victor on August 11, 1929, in Dallas. "Texas Ranger" is a very old song, and it was sung by cowboys as early as the 1830s, when it was often called "The Texas Ranger Boy." The only instrument in the recording by the Cartwright brothers is a sere, droning fiddle, and the lyrics are rawly sweet. There is a plot, full of death and romance and endlessness.

Cowboys were active in the West from the 1820s on. In the late 1880s their numbers began to lessen. Also during the 1880s the mythic cowboy appeared, the forbear of the L.A. yodeler. The first cowboy novel had been published in 1864, *The Hermit of the Colorado Hills* by William Bushnell. Here the cowboys were called herders and given an innocent nobility, not unlike that given to redskins during the Romantic movement of the seventeenth and eighteenth centuries. Cowboy fiction hit its stride in the work of Joseph E. Badger, Jr., who first turned to the West for his inspiration in 1879. Badger's titles included such pukings as *Solemn Saul, the Sad Man from San Saba* and *Daddy Dead-Eye, the Despot of Dew Drop* (yes, there were Dew Drop Inns a hundred years ago).

In *The Cowboy Clan; or, The Tigress of Texas,* an 1891 book by William Levi Taylor, a woman is made to sing the first Hollywood cowboy song.

> *Lie down now cattle, don't heed any rattle,*
> *But quietly rest until morn.*
> *For if you skeedaddle, we'll jump in the saddle*
> *And head you off, sure as you are born.*

During the 1880s cowboys began parodying their own reputations. There are photographs, staged by bored cowboys, of fake lynchings and fake gunfights. Some cowboys became notoriously clothes-conscious; it was not too rare to encounter a sagebrush dandy who had paid two months' wages for a pair of the fancy cowboy boots of soft leather and decorative stitching that appeared in the 1880s.

There are many truisms of the Old West. One was a widespread hatred of cows, a hatred that often birthed sadism. It was not considered odd to rub sand into a cow's eyes to rouse it, or to twist its tail until the cartilage snapped. Jack Clement wrote a song that includes the line, "Some cowboys hate cows, and I'm one of those."

Cowboys disliked niggers also, and Mexicans, who were referred to as greasers. The racism of cowboys was so strong that even a Time-Life book on cowboys (*The Cowboys,* 1973) informs, without qualification, that "the white majority of cowhands were unabashed racists." It is also true, however, that roughly 30 percent of cowboys were either black or Mexican. Several black cowboys, such as Jim Taylor, Jessie Stahl, Nat Love a/k/a Deadwood Dick, Isom Dart, and Cherokee Bill, became quite well known. (Born Cranford Goldsby, Cherokee Bill has been called the black Billy the Kid. Hanged at the age of 20, Cherokee Bill was asked if he had any last words. Bill commented, "I came here to die, not make a speech." His mom claimed the remains.) In 1946 Astor Pictures released a Western musical with a black cast, *Beware,* which featured jump blues artist Louis Jordan, Valerie Black, and Milton Woods, the "colored Basil Rathbone." (Louis Jordan, who was born on July 8, 1908, in Brinkley, Arkansas, and who died on February 4, 1975, in Los Angeles, made several films in addition to *Beware,* such

Louis Jordan and His Orchestra in the 1950s. Left to right, behind Jordan: J. Kirkwood, B. Mitchell, B. Payne, C. Laine, S. Jay, C. Hastings.

Louis Jordan's first album, 1946.

as *Caldonia* and *Shout Sister Shout.* Jordan recorded for Decca from December 1938 until 1954. After Decca he recorded for Aladdin, Vik, X, Mercury, Lou-Wa, Warwick, Melodisc, Tangerine, Pzazz, Black & Blue, and Blues Spectrum.)

Cowboys were known to belch frequently, and to fart, but to yodel? Uh-uh.

Emmett Miller, 2

Emmett Miller sits on a bed. He wears light trousers, light vest, white shirt, and dark bow-tie. He is leaning forward slightly, toward the camera. His left hand rests on his knee. There are a diamond ring and a long, lighted cigar. Close to his right stands a woman, young and thin and pale. Her hair is bobbed. She smiles, but there is a drunken, puffy reluctance in her face. Emmett Miller's arm surrounds the girl's thighs, lifting her skirt almost to her hips. Where his hand holds the inside of her leg, there is another diamond. The girl's thin, silvery garters show above her knees, and her legs are pretty and dully incandescent in her fine silk stockings. Near the girl is a small, low table, on which are three glasses, variously full, and a bottle of Crawford's Five Star. The wallpaper is of a thousand trellised roses.

Emmett Miller has no face. There is a hole in the photograph where it was burned away by a cigarette, a hole of precise and perfect wrath. A piece of chin, a sliver of ear pressed to a girl's hip, one temple and its dark receding hairline—this is all. By the line of the chin and the tightness at the ear and temple, it seems Emmett Miller is smiling.

On the back of the photograph, in crisp, faded blue: "Me and Emmett—Union Square Hotel, New York City—8 / 10 / 28—Sitting on Top of the World!"

I found the photograph, brittle and tawny with its age and its travel, sticking from between pages of *Countries of the World, Vol. II*, in a junk store in Southport, North Carolina, a small ocean place near the bottom of the state. I asked the owner of the store where he had got the book, but he didn't recall. I bought the photo for a nickel.

That was in 1972. A year later it was blown out a ninth-floor window in Manhattan, off the kitchen table of someone I disliked. I watched after it, trying to follow it as it fell, but I didn't see it touch the ground.

Stained Panties and
Coarse Metaphors

In December 1975, Ron Thompson, program director of WWVA, the eminent 50,000-watt country station in Wheeling, West Virginia, dispatched an open letter to the music industry:

"Due to the profanity and distasteful lyrics we have been receiving on records by name artists, WWVA has initiated the following policy. WWVA AM/FM will not air suggestive or profane lyrics. We will delete questionable words and phrases before we play a record. Should the title fail to pass our code of ethics, or if an edit is impossible, the record will not be aired.

"Frankly, we are tired of receiving letters from parents, asking us to explain 'one night stands,' etc. to their children. 'Hell' and 'damn' have become old hat and the sensationalism being used to sell records today has gone too far. It is not our policy to be moral crusaders, but we will not jeopardize our standing in the community. We feel that country music and modern country music stations are the last oasis in the industry. We will not ignore our responsibility to you."

Doc Williams (born Andrew John Smik, Jr., in Cleveland, Ohio, on June 26, 1914), a singer who has performed in WWVA's *Jamboree U.S.A.* since May of 1937, said in an interview with Michael Gast of *The Wheeling News–Register,* "I admit that the risqué titles and lyrics problem comprises less than five percent of the country output today, but I fear that the trend will spread, destroying the purpose and very character of a music form that draws on the best and noblest of the American experience."

117

Program director Thompson and performer Williams were speaking of records such as Tanya Tucker's "Would You Lay with Me (in a Field of Stone)," Conway Twitty's "You've Never Been This Far Before," and Loretta Lynn's "The Pill," hits of 1974 and 1975 that were about fucking. Bob Knight, who succeeded Thompson as WWVA's program director, said the station's antismut campaign met with favorable response, that 350 letters of support and only one letter of opposition had been received.

Like others loud with indignation for the pollution of country music, the folks at WWVA were gravely ignorant of the heritage they claimed to hold so dear. Country music is less sexy, less vulgar than it ever has been. When *Billboard,* on March 25, 1939, published its first list of top-selling Hillbilly Records, it did so with a note that "double-meaning records are purposely omitted from this column." Of the four disks included in that list, two were by Jimmie Davis, one of the most popular, and most intriguing, country singers of the pre-War era.

Born to sharecroppers in Quitman, a small place in northern Louisiana's Jackson Parish, on September 11, 1902, James Houston Davis graduated from the Beech Springs Consolidated School in a class of three. He attended a New Orleans business school after working briefly at a sawmill. He received a B.A. at Louisiana College in Pineville, then went on to Louisiana State University in Baton Rouge. At L.S.U. he became a member of the Tiger Four, a college vocal group that entertained at theaters in Baton Rouge. After receiving his M.A., Davis joined the faculty of Dodd College in Shreveport, where he taught history and social science. Later he became criminal clerk at the Shreveport City Court.

While holding down his civil-service job, Davis also performed regularly at station KWKH in Shreveport. He sang a country music that drew heavily from the blues of the deep South, more heavily even than that of his idol Jimmie Rodgers.

A Victor talent scout was impressed by Davis's performances at KWKH, and on September 19, 1929, a week after his twenty-seventh birthday, Jimmie was brought to Memphis, where he cut 4 songs for Victor. From 1929 to 1933, Davis recorded 68 sides for the company.

OLD FAMILIAR TUNES
AND NOVELTIES

Singing

V-40302 { My Louisiana Girl
My Dixie Sweetheart
Yodeling with Guitars
            Jimmie Davis

V-40299 { On Top of the Hill
Never Leave Your Gal Too Long
with Orchestra
Bud Billings-Carson Robison

V-40300 { Somewhere in Arkansas
The Rambling Woman
with Guitars and Banjo
    Ashley's Melody Makers

V-40303 { Jake Walk Blues
Reckless Night Blues
with Guitar, Banjo and Kazoo
        Allen Brothers

Jimmie Davis

V-40307 { The Story of Freeda Boldt
Sunny Tennessee
with String Band
        Floyd County Ramblers

22523 { High-Powered Mama
In the Jail-House Now—No. 2
Yodeling with Guitar
            Jimmie Rodgers

Jimmie Rodgers

The Music You Want · When You Want it · On Victor Records

Victor catalogue, 1930.

A contemporary of Jimmie Rodgers, Davis was a notable disciple of the elder Victor singer. (Another important follower of Rodgers, Gene Autry, also made his first recordings in 1929.) Like Rodgers, Davis was an urbane, eclectic performer who was influenced by black music as well as by the rural white tradition. Part of Jimmie Davis's repertoire was songs such as "The Baby's Lullaby" and "You're the Picture of Your Mother," frail and wispy stuff of an earlier day. The best and most striking part of his repertoire, however, was a series of songs that dealt with sex plainly or in crypto-lubricities, but never without an extremely raunchy sense of humor.

Much of Jimmie Rodgers's music was sexy ("Blue Yodel No. 9," "Let Me Be Your Side Track," "What's It") and in songs such as "Pistol Packin' Papa" he showed himself to be a master of the wet metaphor:

And if you don't wanna smell my smoke,
Don't monkey with my gun. *

Davis went further than Rodgers. In "Tom Cat and Pussy Blues," recorded in March of 1932, he sang of the heated interactions of "cock and pussy." In "Organ-Grinder Blues," recorded in the same session, Davis sang drolly of impotence and the controversial animal-gland treatment popularized by such charlatans as Kansan John R. Brinkley (who after losing his license to practice medicine in June of 1935, concentrated on operating XERA, his powerful border station in Del Rio, Texas, which broadcast programs by country acts such as the Carter Family). Davis looked to a new tumescence.

Gonna get me some monkey glands,
Be like I used to was;

*"Pistol Packin' Papa" by Jimmie Rodgers and Waldo O'Neal. Copyright © 1931 by Peer International Corporation. Copyright renewed. Used by permission.

Gonna run these mamas down,
Like a Dominicker rooster does. *

In "High Behind Blues," recorded in July 1932, he professes melic lust for dark meat.

When I get to Mexico,
Gonna get me a big, big brown;
No matter how big she is,
I'm the man can hold her down. **

At times Davis borrowed directly from earlier blues records, as in "Sewing Machine Blues."

Gonna telephone to heaven
To send me an angel down;
If you haven't got an angel, St. Peter,
Send me a high-steppin' brown.

He finishes the song with a cheerful leer.

It ain't your fancy walk, gal,
It ain't your vampin' ways;
It's the way you do
Just before the break of day. ***

In "Red Nightgown Blues," cut in August of 1932, Davis fancies himself the object of nymphomaniac attack.

We bought the license,
Went to see Parson Brown;
Corrine couldn't wait
*And she throwed me down. ***

Feminine aggression and much panting ensue. At one point, Davis has Corrine refer to him dearly as "my meat." But perhaps Davis's most unforgettable Victor allusion is in his 1930 recording of "She's a Hum Dum Dinger from Dingersville," where he likens the pelvic torque of his beloved to "a mowin' machine."

In the fall of 1934 Jimmie Davis signed with newly formed Decca Records. In his earliest Decca recordings, Davis sounds as he did in his Victor work; records such as "Shirt Tail Blues," his second release by Decca (October 1934), represent the peak of Davis's Jimmie Rodgers phase. But soon the yodels vanished from Davis's records, and with them the raw vivid instrumentation.

Becoming more of a mainstream artist, Davis made records with Buddy Jones, the Musical Brownies, and Lani McIntire and His Hawaiians. Even Jimmie's voice changed; it got warmer, lighter, and less churlish. At first he did not wholly forsake raunchy material, but what remained of it was greatly toned down. For example, "Mama's Getting Hot and Papa's Getting Cold," released in November 1935, is merely cute. By 1938 the dirty songs had ceased; Jimmie Davis was a crooner.

Davis's first major hit with Decca was "Nobody's Darlin' But Mine," a dark song of death and fidelity vows, released in April 1935. Davis himself recorded three sequels to "Nobody's Darlin' But Mine": "Answer to Nobody's Darlin' But Mine," "That's Why I'm Nobody's Darlin'," and "By the Grave of Nobody's Darlin'." An even bigger hit was "It Makes No Difference Now," written by Floyd Tillman, then a member of the Houston-based Blue Ridge Playboys. First released

*"Red Nightgown Blues" by Jimmie Davis. Copyright © 1932 by Peer International Corporation. Copyright renewed. Used by permission.

by Cliff Bruner's Texas Wanderers on Decca in September 1938, then by Jimmie Davis in November, Tillman's masterpiece of sultry fatalism crossed over to become a national pop hit when Bing Crosby cut it, also for Decca, in 1941. Tillman, however, had sold ownership of the song for a few hundred dollars (he retrieved it when the copyright was renewed in 1966, and today he shares the copyright with Davis).

In 1939 Jimmie Davis and Charles Mitchell, who played steel guitar with Davis, wrote the most popular and most valuable song in the history of country music: "You Are My Sunshine." The song was first cut by the Rice Brothers Gang for Decca and released November 1939. There followed a version by Bob Atcher and Bonnie Blue Eyes on Okeh, and another by the Pine Ridge Boys on Bluebird, then the two best-known country versions: Jimmie Davis's on Decca (released in March 1940) and Gene Autry's on Okeh (released in June 1941). In 1941 Lawrence Welk recorded the song for Decca, and later in the year Bing Crosby cut it for the same label. Since then, no one has been able to maintain a thorough recording history of the song, although Roy Horton of Peer International Corporation, the publisher of the song, contends there is no doubt that "You Are My Sunshine" is the most valuable copyright in country music, the two dubious challengers being Ted Daffan's 1943 "Born To Lose" (also a Peer song) and Pee Wee King's and Redd Stewart's 1948 "Tennessee Waltz" (published by Acuff–Rose).

And here's a precious tale. Lloyd Copas, better known as Cowboy Copas, was one of the most popular country performers in the late 1940s. He recorded for King Records, the Cincinnati independent label operated by Sidney Nathan. Each month, Copas traveled from Cincinnati to Nashville for the purpose of buying songs from writers. When he returned with the songs, Nathan repaid him half of the cost. Copas took authors' rights of the songs, and Nathan took the publishing rights for his Lois Music. One month, Copas returned to Cincinnati with a new batch of songs. He told Nathan that he had refused one good song because the writers wanted too much money for it, $25.

"It's called 'Tennessee Waltz,' " Copas explained, "and all it is, is a

Wesley and Fred Rose, 1950. Photo courtesy of BMI Archives.

copy of Eddy Arnold's 'Missouri Waltz.' And I don't want people goin' around sayin' I'm followin' Eddy Arnold.''

Nathan expressed agreement, but added that maybe, for superstitious reasons, Copas should pick the song up next time he was in Nashville. He gave Copas an extra $10 bill.

Next month Copas returned from Nashville, again without the song. "They sold it, huh?" Nathan asked.

"Well, no, Mr. Nathan," said Copas. "The bastards put the price up to fifty dollars, and I wasn't going to pay that much."

Sid Nathan smiled and patted Copas's back. "You done right," he said. "There ain't no song in the world worth fifty dollars."

In 1938 Jimmie Davis became Shreveport's Commissioner of Public Safety. In 1942 he was made State Public Service Commissioner, a job Huey Long had held. Davis sang his way into both positions.

In 1944 Jimmie Davis was offered the nomination for governor on the Louisiana Democratic ticket. He campaigned for office with "You Are My Sunshine" as his rallying theme. The opposition ran advertisements in newspapers, listing some of his older, profaner songs. (His 1936 "Bed Bug Blues" was called "depraved vulgarity.") Davis won. (This was not the first time country music became an important factor in politics. In 1886 brothers Robert and Alf Taylor ran against each other for governor of Tennessee. Their public debates centered on feral, one-on-one fiddling contests.)

Davis's term of office was not an especially eventful one; Louisiana politics had calmed considerably in the years since Huey Long's death. In 1947 Davis was featured in *Louisiana,* a Monogram film directed by Phil Karlson. Davis's previous B-movies were *Strictly in the Groove,* the 1942 film in which he sang "You Are My Sunshine," and *Frontier Fury,* a 1943 western. His last film was *Square Dance Katy* in 1950.

Charles Mitchell, the steel-playing coauthor of "You Are My Sunshine," was given a government job. Fred Rose was appointed an honorary State Colonel in 1945. Jimmie's term ended in 1948.

In 1960 Davis was again elected to the governorship of Louisiana. Like his opponent, Chep Morrison, Davis ran on a segregationist platform. As in 1944, the dirty songs were dragged from the closet. He

Jimmie Davis campaigning for the Louisiana Primary, 1943.

And to my right, on steel guitar and Public Housing. . . .

Jimmie Davis in the 1960s.

finished his term in 1964. After a fling at running for a third term in 1971, Jimmie Davis left politics.

In the 1950s Davis practically abandoned worldly music for sacred. He left Decca / MCA in December 1973, and signed with Canaan Records, a gospel-music company in Waco, Texas. For Canaan he cut a religious version of "You Are My Sunshine" called "Christ Is My Sunshine." In 1976 Paula Records in Shreveport released his "Walkin' My Blues Away," a strong, bluesy song he had first released on Decca in February 1943. For the most part, however, the Jimmie Davis of the 1970s is a gospel singer.

In the spring of 1976, John Maginnis, editor and publisher of the Baton Rouge tabloid *Gris-Gris,* interviewed Davis at his office in Baton Rouge. Maginnis asked Davis about the sort of music he enjoyed. Country and gospel, Davis answered, "but I don't like country if it's vulgar."

Jimmie Davis was certainly not the first to blend sex and country music. The old British ballads themselves were plump with the stuff, and long before WWVA there were protestors. In 1583 Puritan Philip Stubbes damned balladeers in his *Anatomy of Abuses:* "Their heads are fraught with all kinds of lascivious songs, filthy ballads, scurvy rhimes."

"Tam Lin," "Mary Hamilton," and other ancient ballads refer to abortion. "Gil Brenton" tells of supernatural sheets that broadcast a woman's lack of virginity. The popular seventeenth-century ballad "Fair Margaret and Sweet William" contains the moory couplet:

> *I dreamed my bower was full of red swine,*
> *And my bride-bed full of blood.*

First published in Britain in 1776, "Our Goodman" is the whimsical ballad of a drunken cuckold. Transported across the sea, it became one of the most widespread songs in America. Various versions of it have been recorded commercially by country singers: "Three Nights' Experience" by Gid Tanner and Fate Norris in 1926 for Columbia (but not released); "Three Nights Experience" by John Evans in 1927 for Brunswick; "Three Nights Experience" by Earl Johnson in 1927 for Okeh; "Four Nights Experience" by Clarence Ashley in 1928 for Gennett; "Six Nights Drunk" by Emmett Bankston and Red Henderson in 1928 for Okeh; "Drunkard's Special" by Coley Jones in 1929 for Columbia; "John the Drunkard" by the Carson Robison Trio in 1929 for Perfect; "Johnny the Drunkard" by Asa Martin in 1930 for Gennett; "Three Nights Drunk" by Gid Tanner and Riley Puckett in 1934 for Bluebird; "Old Man Crisp" by the Jolly Boys of Lafayette in 1937 for Decca; "Five Nights Experience" by Mustard and Gravy (Frank Rice and Ernest Stokes) in 1938 for Bluebird; "Three Nights Experience" by Homer and Jethro in 1947 for King. A piece of "Our Goodman" even appears in a Hollywood Western-swing record of 1948, Tex Williams's "Suspicion" on Capitol. It is doubtful that WWVA's standards of decency would allow for the broadcast of any of these disks.

Another British ballad that became very popular in America is "The Foggy Dew," a plain, flowing celebration of skin-thrill that would flush the face of WWVA's program director. In 1930, in Cade's Cove, Blount County, Tennessee, a Mrs. Samuel Harmon sang a version that she called "The Bugaboo" for a guy from the *Journal of American Folklore.*

> *All in the first part of that night,*
> *Me and my love did play;*
> *All in the latter part of that night,*
> *She rolled in my arms till day.*

The first erotic ballad written and published in America is "The Consultation; a new BALLAD, to the tunes of OVER THE WAVES, & JEENY DANG THE WEAVER, and others of equal dignity with the metre," printed in the September 2, 1773, issue of *The Virginia Gazette.* Signed simply "D.C.," the song is about farting, and shitting, too. It ends thus:

> *That dulness, gorged with black ey'd peas,*
> *And feeling foul air rack her,*
> *To give her suffering bowels ease,*
> *Did volley forth a cracker.*

NICK TOSCHES

As echo, without bone or skin,
Exists in verse Nasonian,
So does that fundamental din,
Baptis'd the Muskitonian.
His great descent still in his mind,
He deals in matters squalid,
And sedulous, at each behind,
Announces births more solid.

Is this the stuff of American music's goldener, purer days? Is this essential of Doc Williams's "character of a music form that draws on the best and noblest of the American experience"?

Augustus Summerfield Merrimon (1830–1892) was a United States Senator and Chief Justice of the Supreme Court of North Carolina. As an ambitious young Asheville attorney, Merrimon kept an energetic, often pretentious journal of his activities. In 1931 the *North Carolina Historical Review* published "The A. S. Merrimon Journal, 1853–1854," and in it are some valuable observations of the haveless Southern whites who were creators and lovers of early country music. In the entry for October 17, 1853, Merrimon described the scene at a court session in Jewell Hill, North Carolina.

> *The crowd in attendance were "getting in a weaving way" about night. Some twenty or thirty women were present and most of them were drunk.— I do not know any rival for this place in regard to drunkeness, ignorance, superstition and the most brutal debauchery. I regret that it is so, yet it is true. Scores of women attend the court for the sole purpose of drinking and pandering to the lustful passions of dirty men, and I regret so excee[d]ingly to say, that some men, I will not say gentlemen, are guilty of intercourse with these dirty, filthy strumpets, that ought to be, and one would think they are far above doing such things. . . .*

Merrimon's January 24, 1854, entry gives a similar scene at Yancy County Court.

I saw two women drunk and one cursed and swore desperately and proposed to whip some of her male friends that did not please her. Oh, what a shocking sight to see a woman drunk. A woman! Ah, a woman drunk! Shame on the unfortunate wretch! Infamy and disgrace are indellibly stamped upon the poor creature while she lives, and when she dies the world will be glad to be rid of a hateful pest and mankind soon forget that so mean a being lived. The men too, scores of them, have been drunk. At different times I noticed groups about over the Court Yard and in the center stood a large gauky looking fellow with a fiddle and he would saw off some silly ditty and two or three drunken fools would dance to the same. . . .

Some of the old ballads dealt with the crueler side of sex. The eighteenth-century Scots ballad "Fair Mary Wallington" culminates in death during a cesarean operation.

> *She took out a razor*
> *That was both sharp and fine,*
> *And out of her left side has taken*
> *The heir of Wallington.*
>
> *There is a race in Wallington,*
> *And that I rue full sare;*
> *Tho the cradle it be full spread up,*
> *The bride-bed is left bare.*

Early in the eighteenth century, "The Berkshire Tragedy" came to America. It is still alive in the lingering oral tradition, in a variety of forms: "Knoxville Girl," "The Waco Girl," and others. It is a song of stark, irrational lust murder.

> *We walked along, we talked along,*
> *Till we came to the levellest ground;*
> *I picked me up a stick of wood*
> *And knocked the poor girl down.*

131

She fell upon her bending knees,
Crying, "Lord have mercy on me!
Oh, Willie, oh, Willie, don't murder me now,
For I'm not prepared to die."

Little attention did I pay,
I beat her more and more;
I beat her till the blood run down,—
Her hair was yellow as gold.

This song was cut as "The Knoxville Girl" by the Wilburn Brothers and released in their 1966 Decca album *The Wilburn Brothers Show.* In *Songs That Made America Famous,* issued by Adelphi in 1973, Patrick Sky did a version that he smartly titled "Yonkers Girl" for maximum effect.

Lust murder is also the theme of "The Jealous Lover," called at times "Florella," "Fair Florella," and "Pearl Bryan."

Down on her knees before him
She pleaded for her life;
Deep, deep into her bosom
He plunged that fearful knife.

The ballad "Sir Hugh" has a twist. It tells of the slaying of a young boy by an older woman. Nelstone's Hawaiians (Hubert Nelson and James Touche) cut an eerie steel-guitar version in 1929 for Victor, called "Fatal Flower Garden."

Of all the ancient ballads, perhaps the most striking erotic verse is in "The Knight and Shepherd's Daughter," first published in the eighteenth century. Not "Would You Lay with Me (in a Field of Stone)," nor "You've Never Been This Far Before," nor "The Pill" can approach the plain, moralless lyricism of this ancientry.

He took her by the milk-white hand,
And laid her on the ground,
And when he got his will o' her,
He lift her up again.

Doc Williams is not the only Brown Shirt of innocence in country music. Ray Price (born in Perryville, Texas, on January 12, 1926) was once one of the greatest honky-tonk singers. His earliest records, for the Bullet label, and his work for Columbia throughout the fifties are raw, visceral classics. By the early sixties, Price was becoming more of a pop singer, and by 1963 and his hit recording of "Make the World Go Away," there was more Perry Como in Price's music than Hank Williams, Price's original mentor. Today, Ray Price will tell you that sex belongs in the bedroom, not on the airwaves. The guy's got a way with words.

There are several offensively pious men in country music. Johnny Cash and his God are a particularly tedious act. The strongest drink Cash serves at his parties is nonalcoholic fruit punch. His perspective of country music's history is as surreal as that of WWVA. In the first show of his *Johnny Cash* series, broadcast by CBS in August of 1976, Cash referred to his mother-in-law, Maybelle Carter, as "one of the most influential instrumentalists in country music." Mother Maybelle Carter's influence as a country-music instrumentalist is equal to that of, say, Rudy Vallee. Each year, Johnny Cash's mind seems to grow more monomaniacal. His 1976 hit "Sold Out of Flagpoles" is an absurd mess of godly patriotism, a song berserk with blandness and as dumb as any in the 1975 film *Nashville.*

More ignorable, perhaps, but no less creepy is Roy Acuff. He was born in Maynardsville, Tennessee, on September 15, 1903. This event has been appropriately written of in *King of Country Music: The Life Story of Roy Acuff,* by Acuff's friend A. C. Dunkleberger, published in 1971 by Williams Printing Company in Nashville. Be borne.

In the Smoky Mountains—the GREAT *Smokies, they are called—the peaks seem to stretch higher and higher on all sides around you, and from the tallest ones on a clear day you can see for miles to where the horizon touches three other states. On a clear night you can see a million times as far . . . all the way to the stars.*

Stars of another firmament are not strangers to the Smokies; some have been born there.

John R. Cash

This is the story of a boy, a fiddle, and a dream!
The boy was Roy Acuff. With his fiddle he made his dream come true.
It is an American story—as earthy as the hills of Union County, Tennessee, where he first saw the light of day; an American SUCCESS *story, for such is the harvest of the years we are going to explore.*
Almost it didn't happen. . . .

Good writers make it look so easy! Dunkleberger ends it, 130 pages later.

And so we shall not terminate with a PERIOD *this narrative—this biography of a remarkable career. That would denote finality to something that isn't finished.*
We began by saying "This is the story of a boy, a fiddle and a dream."
It is that—and the dream, while much of it has been fulfilled, still unfolds.
So we shall do the unusual—if not, indeed, the unprecedented—where any book is concerned.
In deference to facts, and to chapters which only time, itself, can write . . . we shall terminate it with a comma—thus

The Acuff biography is not unique among country-music books. Several are as bad, or worse. The first of these junk country books was *My Husband Jimmie Rodgers* by Carrie Rodgers and her friend Dorothy Hendricks (though only Mrs. Rodgers's name appears on the book), published in 1935. The sentences are large, offensive teardrops: "No money for toys! No money to buy—a little white casket." *Hubbin' It: The Life of Bob Wills*, a 1938 book by Ruth Sheldon, was country music's second great contribution to the literature of yech. *Chet Atkins*, a 1967 book by Red O'Donnell of the Nashville *Banner*, is a series of bizarrely truncated paragraphs; reading it is like watching Cheez-Whiz slowly coagulate on someone's chin during lunch. Here is one of Red's finer paragraphs: "A vacation incident in 1966 attests to a guitar's attraction for Atkins." And another, less florid: "Mr. Guitar likes all music." Deep.

Warren B. Causey, who for several years also wrote for the *Banner*, is author of *The Stringbean Murders*, a sort of country-music *In Cold Blood* that was published in 1975. Stringbean, who was born David Akeman in Anneville, Kentucky, on June 17, 1916, was a regular on *Hee Haw* and *The Grand Ole Opry* when he and his wife, Estelle, were murdered by thieves on November 10, 1973. The hero of the story is Tommy Jacobs, the Nashville police detective who solved the case. It isn't a bad book, and there is much grim, gray precision in it: "Police also found three empty beer cans in the kitchen. Three were missing from String-bean's stock of two six-packs in the refrigerator. Raleigh and Marlboro cigarette butts were in the sink." *The Stringbean Murders* also reports what may be the tritest eulogy on record. It is by Maurice O'Neal, Minister of Wingate Church of Christ: "String had a string of friends. Now there is a string of sadness." Death stay thy phantoms.

Not long after the murder of Stringbean, Kinky Friedman and I were sitting at breakfast one Sunday in the restaurant of a Holiday Inn in Houston. There was a quiet, after-church clientele, and Kinky rang a knife against a plate, stood, and solemnly declared, "Someone in this room killed Stringbean." Several persons, who were finished and ready to leave, hesitated lest their departure be interpreted as an admission of guilt. There were no confessions, however, nor quick sprays of gunfire.

There is also a novel about country-music crime, *The Grand Ole Opry Murders* by Marvin Kaye, published in 1974. (The paperback edition spurts, "Down-home hate and blue-grass vengeance when death plays Nashville.") Other country-music novels are *High Lonesome World* by Babs H. Deal, *Heart of Nashville* by Robert Vaughan, and, best of a bad lot, *Ruby Red* by William Price Fox. There's a fuckbook called *Snuff Queen,* but I don't recall the writer's name.

I think the essential country-music prose is found in fan publications such as *Music City News, Country Song Roundup,* and *Country Music.* A piece of writing I shall never forget is "Ray Griff: A Man with Three Countries" by Betty Hofer, published in the December 1974 issue of *Country Song Roundup.* Hofer seems to have studied under Red O'Don-nell, or perhaps the great Dunkleberger himself:

COUNTRY

He's a man with THREE countries.
Canada . . . the U.S. . . . and country music!

Several of the paragraphs include upward of ten words, and one of them begins, "But Bingo!"

The worst country-music writing, however, is found not in the pus-prose of the fan magazines, but in the pale regional publications of New York. In the cover story of the May 17, 1976, issue of *New York*, "Jimmy Carter's Clockwork Campaign Style" by Aaron Latham, the reader is told that to understand Carter he must understand country music. Quotes from several country songs follow, but all the songs are from the film *Nashville*; not merely bad country songs, but fake country songs, written by Hollywood actors such as Henry Gibson. Readers feel the ingestion of a wisdom, and turn to the advertisements of Lucite brie-servers. Would *New York* publish an article on black politician Julian Bond that declared an understanding of blues necessary to an understanding of Bond's political style? An article that compounded bigotry with stupidity by quoting extensively from *Porgy and Bess?* But it is so much more comfortable, so much more acceptable to dislike rednecks than niggers.

Steve Young, a country singer born and raised in Alabama, played guitar in the early sixties for a folksy duet called Richard and Jim. Steve first visited California with them, where he attended the wedding of Richard and Mimi Fariña at the home of Joan Baez, who is Mimi's older sister. Steve recalls that Baez, butterfly of egalitarianism and wet-dream queen of liberals everywhere, was quite repulsed by the presence of a white Southern man. The displacement of hatreds is a droll thing.

The literature of country music has its scholarly side. Magazines such as *John Edwards Memorial Foundation Quarterly* in Los Angeles, *The Journal of Country Music* in Nashville, and *Old Time Music* in London seethe with matrix numbers, abstract obsessiveness, and historical detail. *The Journal of Country Music*, in its summer 1973 issue audaciously printed something called "Esoteric-Exoteric Expectations of Redneck Behavior and Country Music" by Patricia Averill. One paragraph begins, "The same narrowing of options before overt actions and the influence of the S-X factor in that process can be seen in the other components of redneck behavior, and have been illustrated by other people." And you thought all we did was fuck chickens and pray.

The standard country-music history text is Bill C. Malone's *Country Music U.S.A.*, published in 1968. Malone's book was the first, noble lunge out of darkness. *In a Narrow Grave*, Larry McMurtry's 1968 collection of essays on Texas, contained this note: "I had intended to include an essay on hillbilly music, but the impending publication of Mr. Malone's impressive study made such a chapter unnecessary. If anyone knows more about the subject than he does, God help them."

The most beautiful prose written of country music is probably "Some Real American Music" by Emma Bell Miles, a poet, teacher, and mountain woman of Tennessee, who was born in 1879 and died in 1919. "Some Real American Music" was printed in the June 1904 issue of *Harper's Monthly Magazine* and included in her 1905 book, *The Spirit of the Mountains.* Her treatment of country music is perceptive and bare of misknowing romance, and it has lost none of its power in the many years since its publication. In 1975 the University of Tennessee Press in Knoxville produced a facsimile edition of *The Spirit of the Mountains.* It's a precious, eerie thing.

But Bingo!

Roy Acuff made his first records in Chicago in October 1936 for the American Record Corporation. Acuff was brought to ARC by William R. Calaway, an artist-and-repertoire man for the company. A native of Boone, North Carolina, Calaway had worked as a talent scout since the 1920s, and had been associated with the Gennett Record Company of Richmond, Indiana, before joining ARC. At ARC Calaway worked not only with country artists, but also with blues performers such as Charley Patton. Calaway had a bad reputation for stealing the copyrights of his singers. During an eight-year period, he deposited approximately 180 songs with the Copyright Office in Washington, D.C. The last copyright he attempted to register was "The Wabash Cannonball" in 1938. Acuff had cut the song for ARC in 1936, but the Carter Family had recorded the same song for Victor in November 1929 and submitted it for copyright through Southern Music in 1933, the year of its release.

"Almost it didn't happen." Photo courtesy of BMI Archives.

Calaway died in Orlando, Florida, about 1955. Several New York publishers have tried to contact his spirit, but have got no further than a rapping upon a table. The question remains: Is there P.D. after death?

Calaway had been impressed by Acuff's performances, and especially by a song he had heard Acuff sing during his noon radio program at WROL in Knoxville. The song was "The Great Speckled Bird," and Acuff had got it from Charlie Swain, leader of the Black Shirts, a group who also played at WROL. Acuff holds that he had heard bits of the song throughout his youth, and when he heard the Black Shirts perform a complete version, he had Swain write down a copy of the lyrics for him, for which service Swain charged fifty cents.

The melody of "The Great Speckled Bird" is ancient and British. The Carter Family had used it in their 1929 Victor recording "I'm Thinking Tonight of My Blue Eyes." The same melody was used later in the honky-tonk classic "The Wild Side of Life," the mournful and bitter song that Texas songwriter William Warren wrote about his wife. (The song was first cut by Jimmy Heap and the Melody Masters for Imperial. Hank Thompson covered it for Capitol. It was released as a B-side and became the biggest country hit of 1952.)

Folklorist Vance Randolph collected a version of "The Great Speckled Bird" in Pawhuska, Oklahoma, where it was sung as an Assembly of God hymn; and Wilbur J. Cash in his 1941 book, *The Mind of the South*, wrote of "a curious song, entitled 'The Great Speckled Bird of God' and sung quaintly to the tune of 'Blue Eyes,' " that was used as the official hymn of the Church of God.

W. J. Cash was right when he described the song as curious. "The Great Speckled Bird" escapes complete comprehension. The title is from the Bible (Jer. 12:9): "Mine heritage is unto me as a speckled bird, the birds round about are against her; come ye, assemble all beasts of the field, come to devour." This line is one of the great mysteries of Biblical scholarship. One interpretation is that the speckled bird is a vulture. Others see it as a hen attacked by hawks, a bloodied bird, a fine exotic creature attacked for its plumage, or simply a dull fowl. Some scholars have translated the words into English as, "Mine heri-

Jimmy Heap, c. 1955.

tage is unto me as a bird with talons." How could a song rooted in such an abstruse metaphor be anything but curious?

"The Great Speckled Bird" (1937) was Roy Acuff's first hit. It was a great performance and one of the few truly mystical country records ever cut.

SATURDAY'S PROGRAM.

WSM (282.8 Meters).

6:45—Dinner concert by Andrew Jackson hotel orchestra, directed by Beasley Smith (1 hour).

7:15—Bedtime story interlude (¼) hour).

8:00—Barn dance and popular program (3 hours).

WBAW (236 Meters)

4:00—Program presented by the Rigo Manufacturing Co. (1 hour).

5:30—Dinner music from McFadden's (½ hour).

6:00—Organ concert from the Capitol theater by Grace Mitchell and Leon Coles (1 hour).

7:00—United States department of agriculture talk.

WDAD (226 Meters).

11:45 a. m.—Home service talk by Mrs. Gordon Parman (¼ hour).

12:00 m.—Market report (¼ hour).

12:15—Service from Central Church of Christ (½ hour).

9:00—Sweet memory hour (1 hour).

WLAC (226 Meters).

7:00—Elizabeth Edwards Beasley, pianist (1 hour).

8:00—Studio program (1 hour).

SUNDAY'S PROGRAM.

WSM (282.8 Meters).

Silent pending new installations.

WBAW (236 Meters).

1:00 a. m.—Services from the First Baptist church; sermon by Dr. W. F. Powell (1½ hours).

6:00—Atwater Kent Radio Symphony (1 hour).

7:30—Services from the First Baptist church; sermon by Dr. W. F. Powell (1½ hours).

WDAD (226 Meters).

3:00—Singers from the Russell-street Church of Christ.

9:45—Buford Brothers Ensemble.

WLAC (226 Meters).

Silent.

Radio listing, Nashville Banner, December 11, 1926. The Saturday night "barn dance" was not yet called the Grand Ole Opry.

Many of the recordings Acuff made before 1940 were fine country sides, but as time passed Acuff's music became stale and tedious. When he first performed at the Grand Ole Opry in February 1938, the Opry was not too concerned with singers. Since its earliest broadcasts in November 1925 (at first the program was described as only a "barn dance"; late in 1927 it acquired the name Grand Ole Opry), fiddlers and string bands had been the featured performers. There were exceptions. The first and best-known was Uncle Dave Macon (born David Harrison Macon on October 7, 1870, in Smart Station, near McCinnville, Tennessee; he died on March 22, 1952, in Murfreesboro, Tennessee), the singing and banjo-playing vaudeville star who joined the Opry on December 26, 1925. Later there were the Vagabonds (Herald Goodman, Curt Poulton, and Dean Upson), the smooth-crooning trio who joined the Opry in 1931. In 1933 Asher Sizemore and Little Jimmy, his son, came to the Opry; their specialty was mom-death-sin. The Delmore Brothers (Alton, born on December 25, 1908, in Elkmont, Alabama, and Rabon, born on December 3, 1916, also in Elkmont; Rabon died in 1952, Alton in 1964) joined the Opry in the spring of 1933. The Delmores, pioneers of country boogie, made a music characterized by sharp harmonies, hot guitar licks, and wry lyrics. In 1936 Pee Wee King (born on February 18, 1914), a polka-playing Polack from Milwaukee, who led a group called the Golden West Cowboys, came to the Opry. An agent named J. L. Frank was responsible for getting Pee Wee King on the Opry, and it was to Frank that Acuff came after several unsuccessful attempts to perform on the Opry. Frank spoke with David Stone, head of WSM's Artists' Service Bureau, and it was done. Previously Acuff had dealt directly with George Hay, who didn't feel Acuff belonged with the Opry.

Acuff soon became one of the most popular performers on the Opry. More than any other single person, he was responsible for bringing about a reversal of the Opry's original paradigm; never again would the old string bands be as important as the new vocalists and their new and synthetic country songs. From now on, the Opry would reflect the ways of mainstream, commercial country music. (At times the Opry has pretended a vainglory purity, as in its ban on the use of full drum kits during Opry broadcasts.)

Roy Acuff was the avatar of the new Opry, and he loved it. During World War II, Dizzy Dean, a friend of Acuff, started calling him the King of the Hillbillies. This was later changed to the King of Country Music. Acuff reached the apex of his popularity during the forties. Each performance on the Opry of "The Great Speckled Bird," "The Wabash Cannonball," and "Wreck on the Highway" waxed more pompous, as if he were tossing lotus petals of country-music history, or baring a pontifical foot for the kissing. In 1948 Acuff ran for governor of Tennessee as the Republican candidate. He and senatorial candidate Carroll Reece toured the state with a twelve-man band, a portable stage, and two truckloads of props. Reece's speech damned the civil-rights movement and the commies, praised the TVA. Acuff said, "I'm not a politician. I'm just a country boy, trying to run things as honest and square as possible." Tennessee did not bite.

The truth of the matter is that the King of Country Music has not had a Top Ten record in 30 years, and the last time he hit the Top Forty was in 1959. One would tax credibility less by calling Aldo Ray the King of the Cinema. But Acuff has little to worry about financially. In 1942 he put up $25,000 to form Acuff-Rose Publications with Fred Rose, and the company has become the most successful publisher of country music in Nashville.

Roy Acuff enjoys upholding the morals of the United States. John McEuen of the Nitty Gritty Dirt Band, who worked with Acuff and others in the 1971 United Artists album *Will the Circle Be Unbroken*, described the synergy: "Acuff didn't need the money. Wesley Rose talked him into it. He's a little touchy, Acuff. Been in the business like seventy years. He invented the record player. Later he said about us, 'I like those boys, but I can't see 'em with all that hair they got all up around their faces and all.' " Jeff Hanna, also a member of the Nitty Gritty Dirt Band, said, "Acuff made a couple of nasty remarks about Earl Scruggs in front of him. We were sittin' around this big table and Acuff says something about people changin', and then he turns and looks at Earl in a real snide sort of way." McEuen again, "Yeah, right.

Grand Ole Opry Programs

★

With Names of All Performers

All Programs on Station WSM Each Saturday Night

PERFORMERS SUBJECT TO CHANGE

8:00-8:30 P.M.

JAMUP AND HONEY

THE CACKLE SISTERS

UNCLE DAVE MACON, "THE DIXIE DEW DROP"
with Dorris Macon

EDDIE ARNOLD AND HIS TENNES-SEE PLOUGHBOYS
with

Speedy McNatt	Leroy Wiggins
Gabriel Tucker	

BILL MONROE AND HIS BLUE GRASS BOYS
with

Curly Bradshaw	Chubby Wise
Stringbeans	Harold Watts
Tex Willis	Sally Ann Forester

CURLY FOX, TEXAS RUBY AND THE FOX HUNTERS
with

Dempsey Watts	Lloyd George
Tommy Page	Banjo Murphy

8:30-9:00 P.M.

PAUL HOWARD AND HIS ARKANSAS COTTON PICKERS
with

Slim Idaho	Rollin Sullivan
Wayne Watson	Ralph Lamb
	Judy Dean

THE POE SISTERS
Nell and Ruth

CROOK BROTHERS
with

Neal Matthews	Hubert Gregory
Basil Gentry	Blythe Poteet

OSCAR STONE AND HIS POSSUM HUNTERS
with

Oscar Albright	George Ayers
Staley Walton	Walter Liggett
Alcyon Beasley	

PAUL WOMACK AND HIS GULLY JUMPERS
with

Charley Arrington	Burt Hutchinson
James Arrington	W. Roy Hardison

ZEKE CLEMENTS

CLYDE MOODY

9:00-9:30 P.M.

PEE WEE KING AND HIS GOLDEN WEST COWBOYS
with

Becky Barfield	"Spud" Wiggins
Jimmie Wilson	"Spike" Summey
Hal Smith	

ERNEST TUBB AND HIS TEXAS TROUBADOURS
with

Leon Short	Johnnie Sapp
Ray Head	Drake Brothers

GRANDPAPPY WILKERSON AND HIS FRUIT JAR DRINKERS
with

Tom Leffew	Howard Ragsdale
Hubert Gregory	

CURLY WILLIAMS AND HIS GEOR-GIA PEACH PICKERS
with

Sanford Williams	Boots Harris
Joseph Williams	Jimmie Selph
Joe Pope	

9:30-10:00 P.M.

ROY ACUFF AND HIS SMOKY MOUNTAIN BOYS
with

"Oswald" Kirby	Sonny Day
Rachel Watson	Tommy Magness
Jess Esterday	Joe Zinkan

MINNIE PEARL
DUKE OF PADUCAH (Whitey Ford)
MACK McGARR
OLD HICKORY SINGERS
with

Joseph McPherson	Ross Dowden
Claud Sharp	Luther Heathwole

10:00-10:15 P.M.

BILL MONROE AND HIS BLUE GRASS BOYS
with

Curly Bradshaw	Chubby Wise
Stringbeans	Harold Watts
Tex Willis	Sally Ann Forester

10:15-10:30 P.M.

UNCLE DAVE MACON "THE DIXIE DEW DROP"
with Dorris Macon

CURLY WILLIAMS AND HIS GEOR-GIA PEACH PICKERS
with

Sanford Williams	Boots Harris
Joseph Williams	Jimmie Selph
Joe Pope	

OSCAR STONE AND HIS POSSUM HUNTERS
with

Oscar Albright	George Ayers
Staley Walton	Walter Liggett
Alcyon Beasley	

10:30-10:45 P.M.

ROY ACUFF AND HIS SMOKY MOUNTAIN BOYS
with

"Oswald" Kirby	Sonny Day
Rachel Watson	Tommy Magness
Jess Esterday	Joe Zinkan

ZEKE CLEMENTS

10:45-11:00 P.M.

EDDIE ARNOLD AND HIS TENNES-SEE PLOUGHBOYS
with

Speedy McNatt	Leroy Wiggins
Gabriel Tucker	

THE POE SISTERS
Nell and Ruth

CROOK BROTHERS
with

Neal Matthews	Hubert Gregory
Basil Gentry	Blythe Poteet

PAUL WOMACK AND HIS GULLY JUMPERS
with

Charley Arrington	Burt Hutchinson
James Arrington	W. Roy Hardison

11:00-11:15 P.M.

ROY ACUFF AND HIS SMOKY MOUNTAIN BOYS
with

"Oswald" Kirby	Sonny Day
Rachel Watson	Tommy Magness
Jess Esterday	Joe Zinkan

CLYDE MOODY

11:15-11:30 P.M.

ERNEST TUBB AND HIS TEXAS TROUBADOURS
with

Leon Short	Johnnie Sapp
Ray Head	Drake Brothers

ROD BRASFIELD

11:30-11:45 P.M.

PEE WEE KING AND HIS GOLDEN WEST COWBOYS
with

Becky Barfield	Jimmie Wilson
Hal Smith	"Spud" Wiggins
	"Spike" Summey

CURLY FOX, TEXAS RUBY AND THE FOX HUNTERS
with

Tommy Page	Dempsey Watts
Lloyd George	Banjo Murphy

11:45-12:00 M.

PAUL HOWARD AND HIS ARKANSAS COTTON PICKERS
with

Slim Idaho	Ralph Lamb
Rollin Sullivan	Wayne Watson
	Judy Dean

ZEKE CLEMENTS

GRANDPAPPY WILKERSON AND HIS FRUIT JAR DRINKERS
with

Tom Leffew	Howard Ragsdale
Hubert Gregory	

Grand Ole Opry program, February, 1945.

And then we're driving down the street later with Earl, who's one of those very gentle, soft-spoken, old-time country guys, and he turns to me and he says, 'You know, John, that Acuff really burns my ass. He thinks he invented country music.' "

But (quickly, send the children to bed) were you aware that Roy Acuff recorded . . . *smut?* Your pulse quickens, your face horripilates with red. It is true.

At that first recording session in 1936, Acuff and his band cut "When Lulu's Gone" and "Doin' It the Old Fashioned Way," which were issued under the name of the Bang Boys on the Vocalion label late that year. (When the New Lost City Ramblers recorded a 7-inch LP of dirty songs, *Earth Is Earth,* for Folkways in the early 1960s, they took the name of the Bang Boys in commemoration.)

"When Lulu's Gone," rooted in traditional smutsong, is a fast record with a strong bass-line and much heady fiddling.

> *I wish I was a diamond ring upon my Lulu's hand,*
> *Every time she'd take her bath, I'd be a lucky man—*
> *Oh, lordy, bang away my Lulu, bang away good and strong:*
> *What're ya gonna do for bangin' when Lulu's gone?*

How much more interesting than the dullnesses of senescence and yo-yo!

Clarence Tom Ashley (born on September 29, 1895, in Bristol, Tennessee) was, with Dock Walsh, a founder of the Carolina Tar Heels in 1925. About 1932 Ashley performed with Roy Acuff in a medicine-show act (Acuff wore blackface), and it is interesting that Ashley too recorded a Lulu song, "Shout Little Lulu." It was cut in 1966, when Ashley was 71 years old (he died the following year), and released in the Folkways album *Clarence Ashley and Tex Isley.*

> *How many nickels does it take*
> *To see little Lulu's body shake?*
> *It takes a nickel and it takes a dime*
> *To see little Lulu cut her shine.*

The song was also recorded by George Banman Grayson and Henry Whitter in 1928 for Gennett, under the title "Shout Lula." Ashley carried another fine smutsong down through the years. It's called "Farm Girl."

> *I plow her land, and then I sow my seed;*
> *She loves her daddy because I'm long and hard.*

There are more than a few other country songs from the 1920s and '30s that WWVA would hurl. Could Darby and Tarlton's "Ooze Up to Me" even be considered for airplay? What of Fiddlin' Bob Larkin's 1929 Okeh record "Women Wear No Clothes At All"? Or "Hurt No More" by Buster Carter and Preston Young?

> *Just lay down and open it wide*
> *Because I want to rub it a while.*

The early repertoire of Gene Autry was not unlike that of Jimmie Davis. Before he stopped recording smut in the early 1930s, Autry had cut titles such as "Wild Cat Mama," "She's a Low-Down Mama," "She's a Hum-Dum-Dinger" (the Jimmie Davis song), and "Do Right Daddy Blues," which includes the memorable stanza:

> *Now you can feel my legs*
> *And you can feel my thighs,*
> *But if you feel my legs*
> *You gotta ride me high.*

This was recorded for Victor on February 18, 1931. Later these lines emerged in "Don't You Make Me High," cut by Merline Johnson (the Yas-Yas Girl) for Vocalion on October 4, 1938.

Cliff Carlisle, born Clifford Raymond Carlisle on May 6, 1904, in Mount Eden, Kentucky, is one of the finest steel-guitarists in country music, and one of the most exciting old-timey singers. "My music is a cross between hillbilly and blues," he said. "Even Hawaiian music has

147

sort of a blues to it." Of the three great post-Rodgers yodelers (Autry, Carlisle, and Davis), he yodeled the longest and the best. In July 1933, in New York City, Carlisle recorded two songs about defloration for the American Record Corporation, "Sal's Got a Meat Skin" and "Mouse's Ear Blues."

My little mama, she's got a mouse's ear,
My little mama, she's got a mouse's ear,
But she's gonna lose it when I shift my gear.

Gonna take my mouse's ear for a midnight ride,
Gonna take my mouse's ear for a midnight ride,
*Gonna use my old straight eight cuz it's long and wide.**

Carlisle cut many such songs: "My Rockin' Mama" for Bluebird in 1936, "High-Steppin' Mama" for Decca in 1937, and, perhaps his best, "That Nasty Swing," recorded for Bluebird in 1934.

Wind my motor, honey,
I've got a double spring;
Place the needle in that hole
And do that nasty swing.
Yodelayeeyodelayeeyodelayee.

The master of smutsong in the 1930s was a man named Buddy Jones. Not much is known of him. He lived in Shreveport and died there about 1945. He was a close friend of Jimmie Davis and worked in the Shreveport police force while Davis was involved in city government. He recorded for Decca from 1936 to 1942. (His first recordings were duets with Davis.) The band used in most of Jones's sessions was Cliff Bruner's, which went under different names: Cliff Bruner's Texas Wanderers, Cliff Bruner's Boys, and so on.

*"Mouse's Ear Blues" by Cliff Carlisle. Copyright © 1974 by Acuff-Rose Publications, Inc. Used by permission of the publisher. All rights reserved.

Born Clifton L. Bruner on April 25, 1915, in Texas, Cliff started out as a fiddler with Milton Brown and His Musical Brownies in 1936. He formed his own group (Bruner, fiddle; Bob Dunn, electric steel guitar; Moon Mullican, piano; Dickie McBride, guitar; Hezzie Brock, bass; and Will Raley, electric mandolin) and recorded extensively for Decca, under his own name and with Jimmie Davis, Buddy Jones, the Shelton Brothers, and others.

Cliff Bruner's Boys, 1939. Left to right: Moon Mullican, Acee Peveto (steel guitar), Logan Conger, Cliff Bruner, Buddy Dukon, Cotton Plant, KPAC radio announcer.

Cliff Bruner's Texas Wanderers in the 1940s. Left to right: Albert Gonzales, Harris Dodd, Lee Bell, John Wallace, Cliff Bruner, Pete Bumgartner, Buddy Dukon.

Bruner remembers that Buddy Jones was born about 1905 and that the cause of his death was a heart attack. Bruner first met Jones in 1936 when Jimmie Davis came to Houston to record at the Rice Hotel. Davis brought Buddy, and Buddy's brother, Buster, who wrote many of the songs Buddy recorded and played steel guitar at many of his sessions.

Some of the songs Buddy Jones recorded for Decca are "Evil Stingaree" (1938), "She's Sellin' What She Used To Give Away" (1938), "Small Town Mama" (1938), "Butcher Man Blues" (1939), "Rockin' Rollin' Mama" (1939), "Hold It a Little Longer" (1939), "Roughest Gal in Town" (1939), "Easy Rollin' Sue" (1939), and "She's a Hum-Dum-Dinger" (1942). In his best records, Jones is crude and happy. In "Easy Rollin' Mama," he describes his beloved.

> *She rolls her head,*
> *She rolls her eyes,*
> *But she knocks 'em dead*
> *When she rolls her thighs.*

Bruner recalls that Buddy Jones was a quiet man and "very cleancut." He didn't smoke, or drink, or have any bad habits as far as Bruner remembers.

Milton Brown and His Musical Brownies recorded a couple of sexy records in the late 1930s for Decca. One was "Somebody's Been Using That Thing," recorded in 1936. The other, more interesting, record was "Cheesy Breeze," cut in 1935. "Cheesy Breeze" is basically an instrumental, featuring a severely raunchy break by steel-guitarist Bob Dunn, that ends with a very surreal and essentially lewd couplet.

The Tune Wranglers' 1936 Bluebird recording of "Red's Tight like That" was based on the 1928 blues hit "It's Tight like That," recorded by Tampa Red for Vocalion. (Louis Armstrong and Clara Smith both covered the song for Okeh shortly after the original hit. McKinney's Cotton Pickers covered it for Victor.) In the Tune Wranglers' record is one of the strongest lyrics in country music.

> *She couldn't come at all,*
> *She pulled up her stockin' and leaned against the wall.*
> *Oh, it's tight like that.*

"Pussy, Pussy, Pussy" was a minor Western–swing classic, recorded for Vocalion in 1939 by the Light Crust Doughboys, and for Bluebird in 1940 by Bill Boyd and His Cowboy Ramblers. It was a novelty record, a double entendre, not as daring, or as good, as the stuff Davis, Jones, and others had already recorded.

"Truckin'," written by Ted Koehler (author of "Stormy Monday") and Rube Bloom (author of "Fools Rush In"), was one of the most successful songs of 1935. A dance song full of whimsical sexual implications, it was introduced by Cora LaRedd in the twenty-sixth edition of the Cotton Club Parade at the Cotton Club in New York City, and was immediately recorded by many artists. In July and August alone, "Truckin'" was cut by the Mills Blue Rhythm Band, the Little Ramblers, Joe Haymes, Henry Allen, and Duke Ellington. In the months and years that followed "Truckin'," many derivative songs appeared, some of which turned up on country records, such as "Keep On Truckin'" by Smoky Wood and His Wood Chips (Bluebird, 1937), "Can't Nobody Truck Like Me" (written by Moon Mullican) by Cliff Bruner's Texas Wanderers (Decca, 1937), "Everybody's Truckin'" by the Modern Mountaineers (Bluebird, 1937), and "Keep Truckin'" by the Hi Neighbor Boys (Vocalion, 1939). The Modern Mountaineers' record included *that* word.

In his 1947 King record "Let Me Play with Your Poodle" (written by Tampa Red), Hank Penny compared his girlfriend's crotch to "the face of a teddy bear." The record was withdrawn from the market, and a new record (Penny's version of "Open the Door Richard") was issued bearing its catalogue number.

One of my favorite country smut records is "Operation Blues" by Homer Clemons and His Texas Swingbillies, recorded for Blue Bonnet in the late forties, then leased to Modern of Los Angeles.

Now, won't you climb up on this table,
Jerk up that gown.
Raise up that left leg,
Let that right leg down;
Pull off them stockin's,
That silk underwear,
Cuz the doctor's got to cut you, mama,
Don't know where.

In the early fifties dirty country songs were rare. (Ted West's "She Bent My Pole" on Republic, Gene Autry's label, was one of the last glimmers of a fading genre.) But sleazy country songs were common: grim honky-tonk tales of adultery and shame and tears. Welcome to the Age of Guilt!

Rockabilly brought a lot of visceral fun back into country music, but since the early 1960s the sacred sin-guilt-pain schema has dominated the soul of country music: *Lacrimo ergo sum,* and bring the strings up a few decibels.

Who's cutting sexy songs these days? Freddy Weller has done a few. His "Ballad of a Hillbilly Singer," a modest hit early in 1972, had such a strong ending that Columbia released an edited version to radio stations when it became obvious that some program directors simply were not ready for a song in which someone gets his garbanzos shot off. His "Perfect Stranger," a hit in 1973, was softer, but just as sexy —a song of liquor and plain seduction. It is marred, though, by a compromising ending that weakens everything that comes before. "Georgia Girl," another 1973 song, is urbane, literate, and about defloration. (Wake up, Cliff Carlisle!)

Freddy Weller also recorded country music's only lesbian song, "Betty Ann and Shirley Cole," released in his 1973 album *Too Much Monkey Business.* There is not a surface plenty of faggotry in country music, either. But if you ever have the opportunity, hear Cowboy Jack

Derrick's "Truck Drivin' Man," released by King in 1946. In his raspy baritone, Cowboy Jack anticipates the return of his main squeeze:

> *When my truck drivin' man comes back to town,*
> *I'll dress up in my silken gown.*

Shit, you don't hear Johnny Cash singing stuff like *that!* Writer Howie Klein specializes in covering country music for queer magazines such as *Vector,* as well as for "straight" magazines. Howie reviewed Willie Nelson's *Red Headed Stranger* album under the title "Saddle Up": "I'll put Willie's lyrics up against Barry White's as an exponent of the 'gay' experience any day of the week," wrote Howie. Christ, lemme out of here.

A song very close in spirit to the smutsongs of Jimmie Davis and Buddy Jones is Mack Vickery's "Meat Man," recorded by Jerry Lee Lewis in 1973. The words "Maytag tongue" will live on.

We close our lecture on rustic smut with two thoughts. First: "I'm not a prude; I've been around some in my day. But there are things that are sacred in American life. What are we supposed to do, just go . . . FUCK?" (Roy Rogers, *Esquire,* December, 1975). Second: The Country Music Foundation in Nashville possesses two interviews with promoter Oscar Davis (also known as the Baron). In his long and colorful career, Davis had worked intimately with Ernest Tubb, Hank Snow, Roy Acuff, Eddy Arnold, Hank Williams, Elvis Presley (whom Davis introduced to Colonel Tom Parker), and hundreds more. The Country Music Foundation interviews were recorded in July and November of 1974. Davis was in his seventies, partially paralyzed, and he felt the end to be near. He had nothing to lose, and he told it all: a great, glorious, scandalous *Who Fucked Who* of country music, full of homosexuality, pedophilia, and motel drunk-fucks. The CMF allows absolutely no access to these tapes.

And what about dope? Dick Justice recorded a hillbilly version of "Cocaine" for Brunswick in 1929. There is a reference to opium in "Keep on Truckin' " by Smoky Wood and His Wood Chips. "I can sell you morphine, coke, or snow," sings Tommy Duncan in the 1937 recording of "I'm a Ding Dong Daddy from Dumas." (There are other country recordings of "Ding Dong Daddy," such as that of Zeb and Zeke, but none contain this drug line.) The song was written and first performed by Phil Baxter in the summer of 1928. Louis Armstrong cut a hit version of it in 1930, and the Benny Goodman Quartet performed it in the 1937 film *Hollywood Hotel.* Even Arthur Godfrey cut it.

David Allan Coe's "Cocaine Carolina" refers to both cocaine and heroin, and it was cut in 1975 by none other than Johnny Cash.

I think that country music's only timeless contribution to drug music is "Benzedrine Blues," recorded by the Texas Rhythm Boys for Royalty Records at an indeterminable time in the 1940s.

Five years after amphetamine was first synthesized in 1927, Benzedrine was introduced to the pharmaceutical marketplace, and the age of speed began. It soon became a fairly common drug, and magazines enjoyed yelling of its threat to youthful morality. From "Benzedrine Thrill Party," *Whisper* magazine: "The kids become hopped up, not only from the drug but also because they feel they're living dangerously —like those Big Time Broadway–Hollywood heroes do." There is a

From Hello, I'm Johnny Cash, *a Spire Christian Comic by Johnny Cash with Billy Zeoli and Al Hartley. Copyright © 1976 by House of Cash. Published by Fleming H. Revell Company. Used by permission.*

photo: A girl lies dead in nylon stockings and undies. There is a headline: "Idaho Outlaws Benzedrine As Kids Misuse It."

The melody of "Benzedrine Blues" is a familiar one, very similar to
that used by Bill Cox and Cliff Hobbs in their 1937 "Franklin Roose-
velt's Back Again," and by Harvey and Earl Shirky in their 1930 "We
Have Moonshine in the West Virginia Hills."

> *Throw away your Ovaltine,*
> *Buy yourself some Benzedrine,*
> *And roll, roll, roll on down the line.*
> *On down the line,*
> *   On down the line,*
> *On down the line,*
> *   On down the line:*
> *Just take a pill and roll on down the line.*
> *You can go on a coffee diet,*
> *It makes you laugh and dance all night,*
> *It gives you atomic energy.*

At a 1947 Hank Penny session at Castle Studio in Nashville, some-one slipped Benzedrine into Red Foley's Coke. Foley was a boozer, but, unlike many of his Nashville drinking buddies, he was innocent of drugs. His rhythm-guitar work at the session, which produced "Hill-billy Jump," "Got the Louisiana Blues," "Sweet Talkin' Mama," and others, was especially intense. He complained that he couldn't sleep for several days afterward.

Johnny Cash was arrested in El Paso in 1964 for "smuggling and concealing" 688 Dexedrine capsules and 475 Equanil tablets. "I'd talk to the demons," Cash said in 1975, "and they'd talk back to me—and I could *hear* them. I mean, they'd say, 'Go on, John, take twenty more milligrams of Dexedrine, you'll be all right.' "

In 1977 Dr. Landon Snapp of Nashville was brought to trial on twenty-four counts of dispensing Didrex without legitimate medical purpose. Doug Kershaw testified.

Lulu of *Hee Haw* (best leg show on TV) was busted in Dallas in the winter of 1970 for possession of five and a half pounds of reefer. On her wall was a Day-Glo poster of Roy Clark which bore the legend: TAKE MY SEED, DAUGHTER OF THE FEN.

I asked Cliff Bruner if drugs were popular among Western-swing musicians in Texas. He wrote: "This is a hard question to answer. I must say that a very few musicians fooled around with drugs—and when they did, it was controlled more than today. Only marijuana or a 'Bennie' or so—none of the *hard* drugs (heroin, etc.) like today. We had a few 'boozers' but usually under control while playing."

West Virginia Hills Are in the Bronx, Says Barn Barnum

New York, Feb. 27.—Real hillbillies rarely have good night club acts, says Meyer Horowitz, who ought to know. Jewish and Italian hillbillies usually outshine all others on showmanship, he says.

Meyer is the owner of the Village Barn, New York's most successful night club using the homespun motif. Ever since he opened the Barn eight years ago he has been having a tough time finding sock hillbilly acts.

Native-born hillbillies from the sticks usually provide entertaining music, but in most cases they're short on comedy and showmanship. As a result, synthetic hillbillies are as a rule more desirable in a night club than the real ones.

One of his most successful acts was a trio—Annie, Judy and Zeke—all three of Spanish-American descent.

Crockett's Mountaineers followed for a six-month run. They were part Indian. Then came Louis Pope and Nellie Thompson (Italian and Irish), who stayed for six months.

— *Billboard,*
March 4, 1939

You're Going To
Watch Me Kill Her

Spade Cooley was born in 1910 in Grand, Oklahoma. His full name was Donnell Clyde Cooley. During the late 1940s Spade Cooley and His Orchestra was one of the most popular of the California-based Western-swing bands. These California bands were a new sort of Western swing: slicker, closer to the popular swing music of the era, and wholly devoted to large orchestrations. (In 1949 Tex Williams had a harpist, Spike Featherstone, in his band. In the summer of 1948 it was reported that Ted Daffan was leaving Texas for the Coast, where he would organize a 27-piece band, but nothing came of it.) Bob Wills and His Texas Playboys moved to the Coast in 1943, and soon Western-swing dances at Venice Pier and Redondo Beach presented not only Wills, but also a new breed of Western-swing bands, led by men such as Spade Cooley, Tex Williams (who had been the singer in many of Cooley's early records), and Hank Penny. Hank Thompson, who represents an even later, more pop-influenced style of Western swing, recalls seeing Wills and Cooley and others perform at Redondo Beach while he was stationed by the navy in San Pedro during the war. Hank sayas it was not uncommon to see "ten thousand people out at that pier."

Spade Cooley first recorded for Columbia on November 4, 1944, in Hollywood. (He had recorded previously, but only as part of Cal Shrum's band, about 1941.) At his first Columbia session, Cooley cut the biggest hit of his career, "Shame on You," released on January 15, 1945. Cooley stayed with Columbia until 1946. He recorded for RCA-Victor from 1947 to 1950, and then he went to Decca, where he stayed

An early photograph of Spade Cooley's Orchestra. Spade is kneeling on the right; beside him is California radio personality and promoter Foreman Phillips. Second from the right is Jack Williams, later to become famous as Tex Williams (and formerly known by his real name, Sol). Photo courtesy of Doug Green.

until 1955. Cooley was featured in two musical films: *Spade Cooley, King of Western Swing*, a 10-minute short produced in 1945 by Warner Brothers and *Spade Cooley and His Orchestra*, a 35-minute film produced in 1949 by Universal.

In December 1945, Cooley married his second wife, Ella Mae, who was 21 years old. When Cooley had a television program in the 1950s, Ella Mae played fiddle in his band. Cooley had three children: a daughter, born in 1947, and two sons, born in 1933 and 1948 (from his first wife, Ann).

Spade Cooley

Roy Rogers

In 1945, the year of his second marriage, Spade Cooley was arrested for rape in California. He was acquitted.

He retired from television in 1958 and became involved with businessmen in a plan to build a recreational park in the Mojave Desert, called Water Wonderland. The digging of artificial lakes began.

Ella Mae bragged to many of her acquaintances that she fucked Roy Rogers. Spade apparently believed that for a time, but before he died, says Roy, tried to apologize to Roy for having accepted Ella Mae's story. (Spade and Roy were old friends. On several occasions, Cooley worked as a stand-in for Rogers in the younger singer's films.)

On the evening of April 3, 1961, he arrived at his home in Willow Springs, about 85 miles north of L.A. He had been drinking and eating pills. There was an argument. Spade began beating Ella Mae. He forced his daughter to sit.

"You're going to watch me kill her," he said.

Bobbie Bennett, Cooley's female manager, came to the house. Cooley's wife was naked, bruised and red and dying. Her breasts had been burned with a cigarette. Spade stood there, in shock. There was blood on his fancy cowboy boots. The sheriff was called at eleven o'clock.

On April 25 in Bakersfield, a murder indictment was returned against Cooley. He was convicted of first-degree murder, largely on the testimony of his 14-year-old daughter. On August 22 Superior Judge William L. Bradshaw sentenced the King of Western Swing to life imprisonment. As the verdict was read, Cooley slumped. In a cracked voice he said there was nothing he wished to say.

Cooley had written a letter to his friend Hank Penny on April 10, a week after the murder.

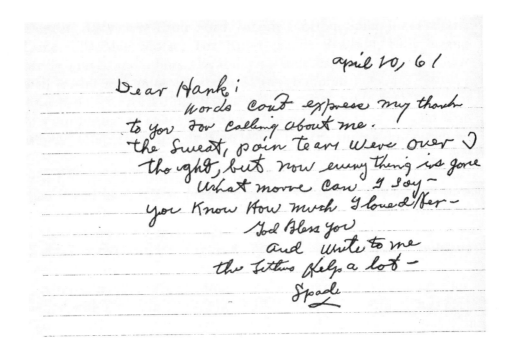

Spade Cooley's letter to Hank Penny.

Cooley sat in Vacaville, a prison 40 miles northeast of Oakland for years. In August 1969, it was announced that he had been granted a parole and that he would be released on February 2, 1970. On November 23, he was granted an evening leave to perform in an Oakland show sponsored by the Alameda County Deputy Sheriffs Association. He was received well and given standing applause. During intermission he collapsed and died of a heart attack.

One of Cooley's last Decca recordings in the 1950s featured a woman, Betsy Gay, singing a song Cooley had written: "You Clobbered Me."

Cowboys and Niggers

Minstrelsy was a Northern love. Its first star was Thomas Dartmouth Rice (1808–1860), a touring actor who parodied the song and steps of an old black stable-worker in Louisville. Rice began performing the "Jim Crow" in 1828. He wrote most of the lyrics around the found refrain:

Wheel about and turn about and do jis so,
Eb'ry time I wheel about I jump Jim Crow.

Rice brought the song back to New York City, and it was a success. He traveled abroad, making "Jim Crow" the first international hit of America when he premiered it in London in 1836. The year before, Alexis de Tocqueville had observed in his *Democracy in America* that "the prejudice of race appears to be stronger in the states which have abolished slavery than in those where it still exists; and nowhere is it so important as in those states where servitude never has been known."

The first minstrel troupe was formed in New York City. The Virginia Minstrels (Dan Emmett, Frank Brower, Dick Pelham, and Billy Whitlock) gave their first performance on February 6, 1843, at the Bowery Amphitheatre. Three months later, the Virginia Minstrels had a six-week engagement in London. Other troupes were organized: the Kentucky Minstrels, the Ring and Parker Minstrels, the Congo Melodists (who became Buckley's New Orleans Serenaders), and the Christy Minstrels.

Southern minstrels were rare. Lew Dockstader was from Hartford,

Dan Emett, author of "Dixie."

Connecticut. Dick José and Honey Boy Evans were from Great Britain. Al Jolson was from New York City. Even Bert Williams, the famous black minstrel, was not of the South.

Minstrelsy lingered into the twentieth century. Issues of *Billboard* in the 1930s still published advertisements for minstrelsy catalogues ("Fast, Furious Fun for Your Minstrel Show"). *Billboard* published a "Minstrelsy" column regularly until June 10, 1939. Then, 23 years later, the Rolling Stones gave us a new sort of minstrelsy. It was minstrelsy without blackface, but minstrelsy just the same.

In the early years of the recording industry, minstrel records were common. Some of Edison's most popular cylinders were minstrelsy: banjoist Vess Ossman's "Darkey Tickle" (1896), "Nigger in a Fit" (1896), and "Little Pickaninnies" (1899); Arthur Collins's "Nigger, Nigger Neber Die" (1899), "Every Race Has a Flag but the Coons" (1900), and "Coonville Cullid Band" (1904); Ada Jones's "Songs My Mammy Sang for Me" (1905), "Bull-Frog and the Coon" (1906), and "If the Man in the Moon Were a Coon" (1906). A 1901 Columbia catalogue lists such minstrelsy records as "De Sweetest 'Backer Is Nigger Twist," "Jolly Darkeys," and "No Coon Can Come Too Black for

How to "Put on" Minstrel Shows

There are many so-called minstrel books on the market. These books are generally stale newspaper clippings thrown together, put into a cover, and advertised as a guide for amateurs. We know of so many cases where the amateur has been fooled that we hesitated when we first conceived the idea that a genuine guide for minstrel shows was badly needed. We realized we had to overcome the bad effects of the many worthless books on the market, but finally decided to go ahead, counting on our past 18 years of honorable dealing with the public to serve as a guarantee that we again offer you the only book of its kind in America.

This book is one of almost 200 pages, and printed from new type o   aper. It tells you everything you want to know about how to "put on" minstrels, and   ᵗⁱᵉ idea that you have never had any experience in this class of work, and carefu¹¹   tle detail.

This book tells you how to select your people among your f·   ge and set the
····ᵍᵉ: how to rehearse your people; how to make up and ᵃ   ving a printed
····   the book. Gives complete wor·   ·sic of   ver composed.
····   ·peusable Opening Medley, †   ·ᵈ-hot opening
····   ·ˢ a howling success for   ·u how to do
····   ·elling you all the   · tells you
····   ·····ʰen and ·   ·ᶠ·nny

Advertisement, c. 1895.

Me." In its 1917 catalogue, Columbia still advertised coon songs, but a bit more demurely. Under the heading Coon Songs, the reader is advised to "See: Negro Songs and Plantation Airs," where he finds airs such as "Nigger Love a Watermelon, Ha! Ha! Ha!" and "I'se Gwine Back to Dixie." The minstrel Bert Williams was an exclusive Columbia artist.

A minstrelsy record of the early 1920s.

In its 1920 catalogue, under Coon Songs and Specialties, Victor printed the following:

NOTE—*By "coon songs" are meant up-to-date comic songs in negro dialect. The humor of many of these songs cannot be called refined, and for that reason we have distinguished them from old-fashioned darky humor, these songs being listed under "Fisk Jubilee Quartet," "Negro Songs," and "Tuskegee."*

Coon songs were usually published by the important New York companies. "All Coons Look Alike to Me," written by a coon, was copyrighted in 1896 by M. Witmark & Sons, the company that published many of Bob Dylan's songs in the 1960s.

Many minstrel songs are found in the repertoires of early country singers. (Some country singers, such as Jimmie Rodgers, Bob Wills, and Roy Acuff, worked as blackface performers early in their careers.) Records such as Fisher Hendley's "Nigger, Will You Work" (Okeh,

A Victor "Darky Specialty" of the early 1920s.

1925), Charlie Parker's and Mack Woolbright's "Give That Nigger Ham" (Columbia, 1927), Uncle Tom Collins's "Every Race Has a Flag but the Coons" (Okeh, 1927), Herschell Brown's "Talking Nigger Blues" (Okeh, 1927), Dr. Smith's Champion Hoss Hair Pullers' "Nigger Baby" (Victor, 1928), Uncle Dave Macon's "The Coon That Had the Razor" (Brunswick, 1928), Earl Johnson's Dixie Entertainers' "Nigger in the Cotton Patch" (Okeh, 1929), and Bill Cox's "Nigger Loves a Watermelon" (Supertone, 1929) were drawn from minstrelsy. After 1930 extremely little minstrel material turned up in country records. Some strikingly atavistic performances are "You're Bound To

JAMUP and HONEY
STARS OF
W S M GRAND OLE OPRY

Jamup and Honey, blackface Opry regulars of the early 1930s.

Look like a Monkey" by Milton Brown and His Musical Brownies (Decca, 1935), Jimmie Revard and His Oklahoma Playboys (Bluebird, 1938), and Hank Penny (RCA-Victor, 1952); "Darktown Poker Club" (written and first recorded by Bert Williams) by Tex Williams (Imperial, 1963); and "Alabama Jubilee" by Jerry Reed (RCA, 1976).

"Run, Nigger, Run" was cut by several early country artists, including Fiddlin' John Carson, who recorded it for Okeh in 1924, and Uncle Dave Macon, who recorded it for Brunswick in 1925. Before either of these records was made, folklorist Dorothy Scarborough found "Run, Nigger, Run" to be common among black Southerners, and in her 1925 book, *On the Trail of Negro Folk-Songs*, she claimed the song went back to the days of slavery. "Run, Nigger, Run" represented a truer kind of musical interaction between black and white, an interaction that had been tamping and defining Southern music since the seventeenth century.

The first important reference to country music in America is the announcement of a fiddling contest in the November 26, 1736, issue of the *Virginia Gazette.*

We hear, from Hanover County, that on Tuesday next, (being St. Andrew's Day,) some merry-dispos'd Gentlemen of the said County, design to celebrate that Festival, by setting up divers Prizes to be contended for in the following Manner, (to wit,) A neat Hunting-Saddle, with a fine Broad-cloth Housing, fring'd and flower'd &c. to be run for (the Quarter) by any Number of Horses and Mares: A fine Cremona Fiddle to be plaid for, by any Number of Country Fiddlers, (Mr. Langford's Scholars excepted:) With divers other considerable Prizes for Dancing, Singing, Foot-ball-play, Jumping, Wrestling &c. particularly a fine pair of Silk Stockings to be given to the handsomest Maid upon the Green, to be judg'd of by the Company. . . .

In the *Virginia Gazette* of October 7, 1737, is this announcement of a fiddling contest, again part of the St. Andrew's Day festivities.

That a Violin by played for by 20 Fiddlers, and to be given to him that shall be adjudged to play the best. No person to have the Liberty of playing unless he brings a Fiddle with him. After the Prize is won, they are all to play together, and each a different Tune; and to be treated by the Company.

Another event of interest was scheduled for that year's festival.

That a Cuire of Ballads be sung for, by a Number of Songsters; the best Songster to have the Prize, and all of them to have Liquor sufficient to clear their Wind-Pipes.

In 1737 appear the earliest references to slave fiddlers. From the *South Carolina Gazette* of September 17, 1737:

Any white person that can play on the violin, or a Negro may be employ'd by the said Logan living in Union Street.

Most of the references to fiddling slaves are found in the advertisement section of the *Virginia Gazette*. From April 23, 1738:

Ran away from the Subscriber in Lancaster County the 17th instant, a dark Mulatto Fellow, named Will: He is a lusty, well-set Fellow, aged about 42 Years; he is pretty much Lock-fretten, and has a Lump on the hind Part of One of his Legs, near his Heel. He wore a Man's Cloth Jacket, a Pair of brown Cotton Breeches, and an Ozenbrig Shirt; he carried with him a white Fustian Jacket, a lopping Ax, and a Fiddle.

From March 27, 1746:

Ran away from the Subscriber, living near James-Town, last Sunday was Fortnight, a Negroe Man, named Henry, who formerly belonged to Col. Charles Grymes, of Richmond County: He is about 5 Feet 6 Inches high, thin visag'd, has small Eyes, and a very large Beard; is about 35 Years old; and plays upon the Fiddle. He had a dark-colour'd cloth-coat, double breasted, flourish'd at the knees, and a blue Great Coat. It is suppos'd he is gone to Richmond County, where he has a Wife. Whoever apprehends him, so that he be brought to me near James-Town, shall have a Pistole Reward, besides what the Law allows. Wilham Newgent.
N.B. As he ran away without any Cause, I desire he may be punish'd by Whipping, as the Law directs.

From April 26, 1776:

Run away from the subscriber in Prince George, the 2nd instant (April) three negro fellows, viz. WILL, DAVIE, and WILL. One of the fellows named Will is near 6 feet high, of a very black complexion, much troubled with fore eyes, and fond of playing the fiddle. Davie is 18 or 19 years old, 5 feet 8 or 9 inches high, of a yellowish complexion, and has what is commonly called a sealled head. Will is about 20 years old, 5 feet 6 or 8 inches high, has a remarkable black smooth skin, a scar on his forehead, and shews his teeth very much when he laughs.

From May 23, 1777:

Run away from the subscriber in Charlotte, the 17th of April last, a negro man named NED, who is a well set fellow, about 29 years old, 5 feet 6 or 7 inches high, has remarkable small legs for his size, walks with his toes much turned out, plays on the violin, pretends sometimes to make fiddles, and is very forward in speaking.

From February 26, 1779:

Run away from the subscriber, on the 26th of May, 1777, a likely Virginia born negro fellow, named HARRY, *about 5 feet 10 or 11 inches high, has been frost bitten and lost some of his toes, two of his fore teeth wide apart, and of a yellowish complexion. I am informed he is lurking about Mr. Joseph Sowell's in Gloucester county, or in that neighborhood; he is very fond of playing the fiddle, and is an artful cunning fellow, and may endeavour to pass for a free man.*

From the *Virginia Herald* of January 21, 1800:

RAN AWAY

On the 25th ultimo, from the subscriber, living near Culpepper Courthouse, A Negro Man named Jack, about 30 years old, 5 feet 10 or 11 inches high, very muscular, full faced, wide nostrils, large eyes, a down look, speaks slowly and wore his hair cued; had on when he eloped, a white shirt, grey broadcloth coat, mixed cassimere waistcoat and breeches, a brown hat, faced underneath with green, and a pair of boots. He formerly belonged to Mr. Augustin Baughan, of Fredericksburg, now of Baltimore, and I am told was seen making for Alexandria, with the intention of taking the stage thither: he is artful and can both read and write and is a good fiddler.

This was not too long ago, a mere life-span before the births of men such as Uncle Dave Macon (1870) and W. C. Handy (1873), a mere life-span before the phonograph. In the July 25, 1774, entry of *The Journal of Nicholas Cresswell, 1774–1777,* the 23-year-old Englishman described a Southern party. The picture is one that did not fade until the twentieth century.

About noon a Pilot Boat came along side to invite the Captn. to a Barbecue. I went with him and have been highly diverted. These Barbecues are Hogs, roasted whole. This was under a large Tree. A great number of young people met together with a Fiddle and Banjo played by two Negroes, with Plenty of Toddy, which both Men and Women seem to be very fond of. I believe they have danced and drunk till there are few sober people amongst them. I am sorry I was not able to join them. Got on board late.

The fiddle was the most common musical tool among both whites and blacks throughout the nineteenth century. One of the first New Orleans balls, described in 1802, featured a band of 6 black musicians, most of whom played fiddles. A directory of 217 jazz musicians who worked in the Storyville district of New Orleans between January 1, 1898, and November 17, 1917, reveals that there were more fiddlers in these early jazz bands than trumpeters, banjoists, or saxophonists. In *Blues: An Anthology,* W. C. Handy tells that his original band, organized in the first decade of this century, consisted of a cornetist (Handy), a saxophonist, a clarinetist, a trombonist, a guitarist, a bass-player, and three fiddlers (Ed and Paul Wyer and Jim Turner). The song version of "Memphis Blues" (the original, copyrighted in 1912, was purely instrumental), published in 1913, refers to a jazz fiddler.

In her 1942 book, *Slave Songs of the Georgia Sea Islands*, Lydia Parrish wrote of her encounter in 1932 with Green Harris, a black fiddler who was born in 1856. Harris told her that the fiddle, although sinful, was the favored instrument of Southern blacks.

Leroy Parker, who played in Mamie Smith's second session, on February 14, 1920, in New York City, was the first blues fiddler to record. In 1922 George Bell replaced Parker as fiddler in Mamie's records. Fiddler Armand J. Piron and his New Orleans Orchestra first recorded in 1923. Bessie Smith recorded with fiddler Robert Robbins in 1924. In 1925 blues singer Clara Smith cut a song with fiddler Leon Abbey; that same year, blues fiddler Lonnie Johnson made his first records. Jelly Roll Morton recorded with a pair of fiddlers in 1926. Peg Leg Howell used Eddie Anthony on fiddle in some 1927 recordings. In 1929 Charley Patton recorded with fiddler Henry Sims, who cut two records under his own name that year, using Patton on guitar. In 1930 the Mississippi Sheiks, a black group that featured much fiddling, made their first records. In 1942 Muddy Waters sang in several recordings by the Son Simms Four, the leader of whom, Son Simms, was a Mississippi fiddler and, some think, the same man who had accompanied Charley Patton 12 years before. The black fiddling tradition lingers. In 1972 fiddler Claude Williams, who was born in 1908 in Oklahoma, cut a beautiful and not at all archaic album with pianist Jay McShann for

HUNDREDS TURNED AWAY LAST NIGHT

Bijou Theater

Another Special Show for White People

TONIGHT 10:30 p.m.

Regular Show 8:30—Colored Only

"CHARLESTON DANDIES"

40 PEOPLE—JAZZ BAND

"Passed by the Board of Censorship"

PHONE 6-5981 FOR SEATS

Advertisement, Nashville Banner, *November 27, 1926.*

Advertisement, Nashville Banner, *November 13, 1926.*

Sackville Records, a small Canadian company. Williams was the fiddler with Andy Kirk and His Twelve Clouds of Joy in the 1920s and '30s.

Black fiddle music was not too different from its white source. Henry Sims's style of fiddling with Charley Patton, who had a wholly black vocal style, is like the work of many white country fiddlers of the day. It is rawer and empty of the speed and tremolo of Mississippi fiddle bands such as the Leake County Revelers, Ming's Pep Steppers, the Mississippi Possum Hunters, Narmour & Smith, and the Ray Brothers, but its tones are plain proof of a century of cultural seepage in Mississippi, a century of windings and flowings that spilled onto the lap of the 1920s both Henry Sims and the Mississippi Possum Hunters.

Sam Chatman, guitarist with the Mississippi Sheiks, recalled that ''my father, he played the fiddle—old songs like 'Turkey in the Straw' and such.'' Honeyboy Edwards, born in 1915 in Itta Bena, Mississippi, is another blues singer whose father played fiddle. Skip James, born in 1902 in Bentola, Mississippi, recalls attending country dances where a black man named Green McCloud fiddled. Fred McDowell, born about 1905 in Rossville, Mississippi, also remembers black fiddlers playing at dances. Gatemouth Brown, born in 1914 in Vinton, Louisiana (but raised in Texas), played fiddle before he took to the guitar. Brown includes modern country songs, such as Johnny Horton's ''The Battle of New Orleans,'' in his performances.

Butch Cage (born James Cage on March 16, 1894, near Meadville, Mississippi) was a black fiddler who recorded by himself and with other blues singers. Cage held the fiddle to his chest as he played, a style favored by old-timey country fiddlers such as Eck Robertson. Cage remembered two other black fiddlers he knew in Franklin County, Mississippi: Frank Felters and Old Man Carol Williams. As a young man, Cage heard the older fiddlers perform "Arkansas Traveler," "Hell Broke Loose in Georgia," "Old Wagoner," and other songs associated with white fiddling.

Bijou Theater, Thurs., Dec. 16

"SHUFFLIN' SAM FROM ALABAM'"

35 PEOPLE—JAZZ BAND

Regular Show 8:30—Colored Only

SPECIAL SHOW FOR WHITE PEOPLE **10:45**

"Passed by the Board of Censorship"

PHONE 6-5981 FOR SEATS

Advertisement, Nashville Banner, *December 13, 1926.*

Guitars had been played in America since the eighteenth century, but it was not until the latter part of the next century that they became commoner than fiddles among rural musicians. The rise of the guitar was part economic and part religious. It was easier to build and maintain than the fiddle, and it was less frowned upon by religious groups, especially black, who had used the fiddle as a goat's-ass symbol of sin since early in the 1700s.

The technique of slide-guitar playing, associated with blues musicians, and that of steel guitar, associated with country musicians, have a common source in popular Hawaiian music of the late nineteenth century. The guitar was probably introduced to the Hawaiian Islands by Spanish and Portuguese sailors and Mexican cowboys who were brought in when cattle ranching became an important industry, but it did not become an integral part of Hawaiian music until after 1879, when a group of Portuguese immigrants, three of whom were instrument makers, arrived from Madeira.

The Hawaiian guitar style, forerunner of the American slide and steel styles, centered on the use of a hard, smooth object upon the strings to effect a slithery, airy sound, an exaggerated glissando, instead of the defined notation of finger stops. The Hawaiian style is said to have been invented by Joseph Kekuku, a student at the Kamehameha Boys School in Oahu, about 1894. Kekuku discovered the effect of using a comb or a knife on the strings of his guitar, then used a metal bar for even greater effect. His invention caught on quickly. It is difficult to believe that no one in the history of Western civilization toyed with the effects of odd objects upon a guitar's strings before Kekuku came along, but he must remain the documented, and in his own day uncontested, inventor of the Hawaiian guitar style.

The style came to America in the 1890s and took the attention of the pop masses as yodeling had years before. W. C. Handy recalled seeing a black man play upon his guitar's strings with the blade of a knife in 1903.

By 1920 the record companies were deeply involved in Hawaiian guitar music. The most popular artists were Louise & Ferera (the husband-wife team who recorded for Brunswick, Columbia, and Victor), the Toots Paka Hawaiian Company, Lua & Kaili, and the Hawaiian Quintette. Some of these performers, such as Pale K. Lua and David Kaili, were real Hawaiians, but others, such as Frank Ferera, the most famous of the early Hawaiian guitarists, were not. (Ferera was a Portuguese cowboy. He came to America with the troupe of Keoki E. Awai to entertain at the Panama Pacific Exposition in 1914, and soon he and his wife, Helen Louise, began recording.)

Sol Hoopii, often considered the best and most important Hawaiian guitarist, came to America in 1919. In 1925 he formed a group with Lani McIntire and Glennwood Leslie, and the group began recording for Columbia. Hoopii appeared in several films: *Bird of Paradise*, *Flirtation Walk*, *Sing Me a Song of the Islands*, *Waikiki Wedding*, and many

Charlie Chan episodes. In 1938 he became an evangelist, and on November 16, 1953, he died.

Hawaiian guitar music was popular until the late 1940s. Decca's 1942 popular catalogue listed more than 500 Hawaiian titles. Two Decca artists, Bing Crosby and Jimmie Davis, recorded sessions with Lani McIntire and His Hawaiians. (Crosby appeared with Hoopii in *Waikiki Wedding.*)

The first blues guitarist to record in a Hawaiian-derived style was Blind Lemon Jefferson (1897–1930), who played slide guitar in "Jack o' Diamond Blues" in May 1926. Lemon (and this was his given name; he had an older brother named Izakiah) was born blind in Couchman, Texas, a small place near Mexia that is no longer found on maps. He made his living in the red-light district of Dallas. Jefferson was a grotesque creature, a beastly fat man who cared for nothing but cunt and whiskey. J. Mayo Williams, the recording manager of Paramount's race division, knew Jefferson's needs, and after each session he paid the blind man his due: a few paper dollars, a bottle of bootleg whiskey, and a whore who didn't sound at Lemon's dull lumberings.

Blues guitarists throughout the South fitted metal tubes or bottlenecks onto their fingers, like Blind Lemon Jefferson. The sound was usually not too different from that produced by the Hawaiian guitarists. It was less tied to melody than to interpolation, and it was raunchier. The blues guitarists never favored the Hawaiian custom of resting the guitar flat upon the lap, but held to the Spanish position. One of the few bluesmen who played lap-style was Bukka White (1909–1977).

In the 1930s the influence of the Hawaiian guitarists had changed the sound of the blues. The slide style became a watermark of both rural and urban bluesmen, a ubiquitous sound that was no less common in the Mississippi Delta than in Chicago. Bluesman Casey Bill Weldon was billed on some of his records as the Hawaiian Guitar Wizard. One of the most effective slide guitarists of those years was Scrapper Blackwell, who recorded with the Nashville pianist and singer Leroy Carr in the late 1920s and early '30s.

In 1954 Elmore James, a master of the electric slide guitar who was born in Canton, Mississippi, on January 18, 1918, and died in Chicago on May 23, 1963, recorded a tribute to his musical roots for Flair Records in Chicago. It was called "Hawaiian Boogie."

Five months after Blind Lemon Jefferson made his first slide guitar records in 1926, Frank Hutchison, a white man born in Raleigh County, West Virginia, on March 20, 1897, became the first country performer to record in the same style. This was in New York in October 1926, and the session resulted in Hutchison's first Okeh single, "Worried Blues" c / w "Train That Carried the Girl from Town." Hutchison held his guitar in the Hawaiian fashion, as would many country musicians after him. His style was cleaner, faster, and more concerned with harmonics than that of Blind Lemon. Hutchison recorded until September 1929, then worked as a steamboat entertainer and store owner. He died on November 9, 1945.

Frank Hutchison's "K.C. Blues," cut in New York City on June 9, 1929, is one of the most precious of the old-timey country records, not merely for its splendid guitar work, but also for an occurrence halfway through it. To Hutchison's mind, the song is ended. There is a small silence as the men from Okeh signal that he must continue, that the record must be longer than the minute and 50 seconds he has given them. Hutchison's solution is to speak.

"All right, boys. This is Frank Hutchison, settin' back in the Union Square *Ho*tel, just gettin' right on the good corn liquor."

Then he resumed playing. It was the time of Prohibition, but Okeh released the record anyway.

Black guitarists called their Hawaiian-derived style "slide" or "bottleneck," but country musicians called it "steel." In the mid 1920s the Dopera Brothers, Ed and Rudy, manufactured their all-metal National guitar, and in 1929 they produced the first wood-and-metal dobro. Both guitars were constructed with aluminum resonator disks (the National had three, the dobro one) to effect natural amplification. Patents were licensed to several firms to make dobros. Although many black musicians used Dopera guitars, these guitars were most popular among country musicians.

Darby and Tarlton made their first records in 1927. Jimmy Tarlton, born on May 8, 1892, in Chesterfield County, South Carolina, adopted the bottleneck style in 1902 after observing its use by black guitarists. He began using a steel bar in 1923, when he saw Frank Ferera perform in California, and he settled upon the use of an automobile wrist-pin in the late 1920s. Tarlton played a National guitar in most of his recordings. Like many other country artists of the 1920s and '30s, Darby and Tarlton made a severely black-sounding music. Some of their records, such as "Slow Wicked Blues," would be barely recognizable as the stuff of white boys were it not for Tarlton's yodeling.

Cliff Carlisle, who first recorded in 1933, was also very influenced by blues. Carlisle was a more emphatic, more urbane steel-guitarist than Tarlton. Carlisle's tough, swooning steel work was the perfect complement to the raunchy double-entendre songs that were his specialty.

Jimmie Rodgers, who made black music accessible to white audiences, used many steel-guitarists in his sessions: E. T. Cozzens (the first, in February 1928), John Westbrook, Lani McIntire, and others. His

August 1929 recording of "Everybody Does It in Hawaii" featured a trio of steel-guitarists, perhaps Sol Hoopii's group. The following December, King Oliver and His Orchestra cut the song. In May 1931, Rodgers cut a new version of "Everybody Does It in Hawaii," again with three steel guitars. This recording was issued in "Jimmie Rodgers' Puzzle Record," a disk that had three different lead-in grooves. Each time you put the needle to the record, you heard one of three recordings (the other two were "Blue Yodel" and "Train Whistle Blues") that had been pressed onto a single disk in parallel grooves. The first such record had been issued by Victor about 1920; it was called "The Conundrum (What Will I Play Next)" and described in the Victor catalogue as "Four short selections, any one of which the needle may decide to play." In 1975 Arista issued an album by Monty Python, *Matching Tie and Handkerchief*, that had two different lead-in grooves on one of its sides. It was wrongly advertised as the world's first three-sided record.

Roy Harvey of Beckley, West Virginia, who recorded with Charlie Poole's North Carolina Ramblers from 1926 to 1929, and with various other artists during the same period, was a steel-guitarist of extreme subtlety. He recorded "Guitar Rag" as a duet with Jesse Jackson, another West Virginia guitarist, in 1930 for Brunswick. ("Guitar Rag" was a steel-guitar version of a song by the same name that Sylvester Weaver, an obscure blues musician, recorded for Okeh in 1923.) The Hokum Boys cut it in 1931 for Romeo. Leon McAuliffe used the title "Steel Guitar Rag" when he cut it with Bob Wills and His Texas Playboys in 1936.

One of the greatest popularizers of the dobro sound was James Clell Summey (1914–1975), who joined Roy Acuff in 1933. Acuff called this group, which included three other men, the Tennessee Crackerjacks. In 1935 he changed the group's name to the Crazy Tennesseeans, a misspelling he used for his early records. Summey's dobro work is responsible for the strong, haunting quality of Acuff's earliest and best records. Two of his finest dobro performances were cut at Acuff's March 1937 session: "Steel Guitar Chimes" and "Steel Guitar Blues." Summey quit Acuff in January 1939 (in this same month Acuff changed the name of his group to the Smoky Mountain Boys; Harry Stone, the manager of WSM, felt the old name was too derogatory) and was replaced by Pete Kirby, or Bashful Brother Oswald. By that time, the steel guitar had replaced the fiddle as the signature instrument of country music.

Some country singers experimented with the steel-guitar sound in their recordings, but returned to the plainer sound of standard guitar accompaniment. Gene Autry was one of these singers. In 1931 he cut several songs with steel-guitarist Frankie Marvin, who had recorded on his own for Edison, Brunswick, and other labels, and with his brother as Frankie and Johnny.

Some older artists still use dobros in their bands, and in the late 1970s a few younger singers, such as David Allan Coe and Tompall Glaser, got a striking sound in their records by using dobros instead of more modern steel guitars. But what is commonly called the steel guitar today is a drastically different instrument, a drastically different sound.

The first electric lap steel was manufactured by Rickenbacker in 1931. By 1935 several country steel-guitarists were using amplified guitars, usually acoustic models with electrical pick-ups. Unlike most dobro-players, the first amplified guitar-players held the instrument in the Spanish position. Bob Dunn was probably the first amplified steel-guitarist. He joined Milton Brown and His Musical Brownies late in 1934 (he had toured with vaudeville bands since 1927) and added a severe new energy to the group's records when he started recording with them in January 1935 at the band's second session. (The Brownies had first recorded on April 4, 1934, at the Texas Hotel in San Antonio.) Cliff Bruner remembers Dunn's guitar to have been a mongrel of wood and metal.

"He had an old guitar he picked up down in Mexico, a Mexican guitar that had a homemade pick-up on it. And he would have to magnetize his strings. He carried a magnet with him. He used this magnet to magnetize the strings, and he had a homemade pick-up built to go on it. Bad amplifiers, too, at those times."

Bob Dunn was the lord of the steel guitar. In the 1930s he wrought a music full of electric wonders. Great yelling dissonances burst from his bastard tool like glass against a stone wall. Three years before Django Reinhardt made his first records, Dunn had a style as subtle and involved as Reinhardt's would be, but Dunn had a daring, febrile energy that neither Reinhardt nor the effete jazzbos who came in his wake could comprehend. Today there are people who hear the influence of Django Reinhardt in Bob Dunn's music, as if it were unthinkable that this gentle Texas redneck could create such a music on his own.

Dunn's best work was in such Brownies records as "Cheesy Breeze," "Who's Sorry Now," "You're Tired of Me" (all cut in 1935), and "Somebody's Been Using That Thing" and "Yes Sir!" (both cut in 1936), where he mixed loud, lucid notes with fast, jagged triplets and grabbed at variously toned shreds of melody that complemented the song with bizarre, lizard-eye concision. These solos lunged like drunks, or rushed, graceful like hawks, from here to there to here. He even made "Shine on Harvest Moon" sound dirty.

Milton Brown was severely injured in a car wreck on the night of April 13, 1936, as he was driving to Fort Worth from Crystal Springs on the Jacksboro Highway. He was brought to a hospital, but complications arose and he died on April 18, at the age of 32. Such was his local popularity that 3500 people came to the funeral. Cliff Bruner, who had joined the Brownies in 1936, thinks Brown's death could have been prevented.

"He had a punctured lung, and they had the old family doctor. A new doctor came in and said, 'If you let me, I'll save Milton's life.' See, it wasn't all that serious. He's sittin' up in bed talkin' to me the next morning. And they let pneumonia set in, and this was before pennicillin and all that. He'd just had a punctured lung; pneumonia set in and killed him. It was uncalled for, actually.

"At that time, he had the number one band. After his death, his brother tried to keep the group together, but he just didn't have the leadership. I'd have never left Milton, I'd have never had a band of my own if Milton had lived. I'd have been happy just working in his band, 'cause he was the greatest.''

After the Brownies broke up in 1936, Bob Dunn started recording for Decca with his own group, the Vagabonds, and with Cliff Bruner's bands. Some of his Vagabond recordings, such as "Blue Skies" and "Toodle-Doodle-Oo," a derivative of "It's Tight like That," were as good as any of his work with the Brownies, and his work with Cliff Bruner produced many of Western swing's raunchiest and best records. In the 1930s Western-swing musicians in Texas interacted so much that the recording histories of many of the most important men, such as Dunn, are hard to unravel. A good example is "Two More Years" by Leon Selph's Blue Ridge Playboys, released by Decca in 1938. In reality, Leon Selph was nowhere in sight when "Two More Years" was cut, for he was in trouble with the musician's union at the time. The vocal was by Floyd Tillman, who was in the Blue Ridge Playboys, but the other musicians included Cliff Bruner on fiddle, Bob Dunn on steel guitar, and Moon Mullican on piano, all of whom were in the Texas Wanderers, Bruner's band.

Bob Dunn stopped recording in the 1940s, after which he taught music and operated a music store in Houston. According to Cliff Bruner, Dunn died about 1970.

St. Louis Blues
Sweet Jennie Lee
Texas Hambone Blues
Brownie Special
Right or Wrong
Washington And Lee Swing
Beautiful Texas
Little Betty Brown

Milton Brown's only LP, released 20 years after the band's last session.

"He had retired. He'd taught a lot. Y'know, Bob had a master's degree in music. Possibly his doctor's degree. He was a graduate of the Conservatory here in Houston. He was a very finished musician, and he taught a long time. He had a big music store, a big business, and he sold it and was going to retire and enjoy his earnings, and he found

189

Cliff Bruner's Boys, 1940. Left to right: Harris Dodd, Logan Conger, Cliff Bruner, Buddy Dukon, Eddie Caldwell, Curly DeLouche, Link Davis, Johnny Thames.

out he had cancer. It was a terrible thing. Dickie McBride died one day and Bob died the next day, both in the same hospital. One on the first floor and one on the second. A real tragedy.

"I always considered Bob a genius. He was futuristic, that's the way Bob was. He originated the whole thing. He was a wonderful guy, one of the nicest guys that ever lived. He was, you know, caught takin' a drink once in a while, but he quit that in his older days. He was a nice guy."

There are other tales of Bob Dunn's being caught taking a drink.

One Western-swing veteran said it was always wise to bring a back-up steel-guitarist with you when you played a date with Dunn, just in case he wilted off his chair in the middle of a set.

After Dunn's first recordings with the Brownies, amplified steel playing flourished in Texas. Ted Daffan (born Theron Eugene Daffan on September 21, 1912, in Beauregarde Parish, Louisiana) recorded with Shelly Lee Alley and His Alley Cats and Leon Selph's Bar-X Cowboys (both Houston bands) before forming his own band in 1939. Daffan wrote and recorded the classic "Born To Lose" for Okeh in 1943.

"I was nineteen years old when I first saw the Hawaiian guitar played. A cousin of mine who played standard had come down from New Orleans to visit us in Houston. He was working with a local Houston boy named Clayton Wilson, and Clayton played the steel guitar. That was the first time I'd ever seen it played, and I fell in love with it. I immediately bought a five-dollar guitar at a pawnshop and got a fifty-cent instruction book and started in. This was during the Depression; there was no money for lessons or training, anything like that. But I did teach myself to read, write, and arrange.

"In '33 I was playing Hawaiian music and I had a group called the Blue Islanders on KTRH. In '34 I started playing steel with a little group here in Houston called the Blue Ridge Playboys. About a year later, I joined the Bar-X Cowboys.

"The amplifiers with pick-ups had just come on the market, so I immediately purchased one. That was one of the first ones on the market. It was called a Volatone. It was necessary in order to play dance jobs. I first played one late in '34. I first recorded with an electric steel in December of '39.

"After I had turned country, there was a great steel player working with Milton Brown and His Brownies, called Bob Dunn. I admired his steel playing terrifically, but I could never duplicate it. He had a very individualist style, and I never even tried. I stuck mostly to straight lead. He played a very sophisticated jazz steel. Bob Wills, of course, had a great steel player, Leon McAuliffe."

Al Dexter was born Albert Poindexter on May 4, 1902, in Jacksonville, Texas. His 1943 recording of "Pistol Packin' Mama" for Okeh was the biggest selling record of the year. Within six months of its release, the record sold a million copies, and sheet music sales hit 200,000. The Duke of Windsor was caught humming it, *Life* called it "a national earache," jukebox operators during the Petrillo Ban (a strike by the American Federation of Musicians that crippled the record business in 1942 and 1943) paid as much as $10 for a black-market copy of it, Frank Sinatra sang it for 14 weeks straight on *Your Hit Parade*, and Bing Crosby had one of the biggest hits of the decade when he covered it for Decca. The song also entered folk tradition (in her 1961 Folkways album, Aunt Molly Jackson of Kentucky sang it and claimed she was its source) and was revived in a rockabilly version by Mac Curtis in 1975.

Al Dexter never heard of Aunt Molly Jackson. (It is not too uncommon for pop hits to be collected in the hills by folklorists. In 1959 D. K. Wilgus, Professor of English and Anglo-American Folksong at U.C.L.A., recorded performances of Bill Justis's "Raunchy" and the Everly Brothers' "Bye Bye Love" by the Sammie Walker Family of Summer Shade, Kentucky. In June 1965, Wilgus recorded a hot "Blue Suede Shoes" by Aunt Ollie Gilbert of Mountain View, Arkansas.) In 1975 Dexter told me the story of his million-dollar song.

"I used to go sit around these honky-tonks, beer joints. At one time I owned a tavern, the Round-Up Club, in Turnertown, Texas. I had a

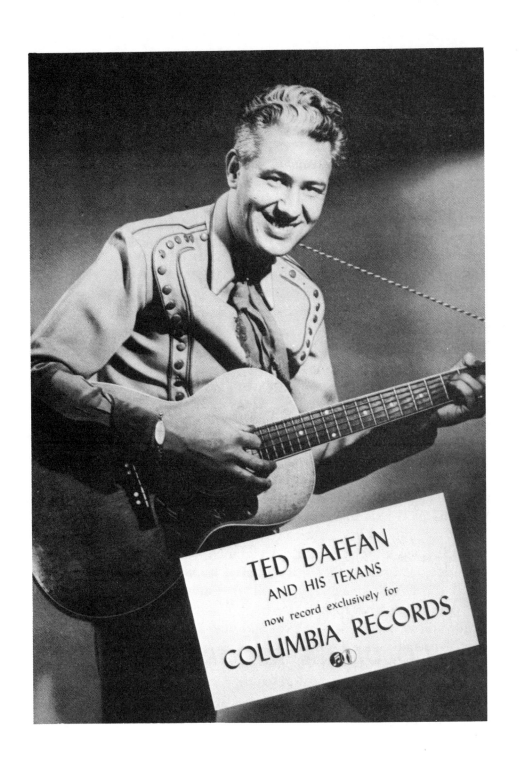

TED DAFFAN
AND HIS TEXANS
now record exclusively for
COLUMBIA RECORDS

bunch of girls workin', and there was a little cross-eyed feller who brought a girl in one night by the name of Jo Ann, and he asked me if I'd give her a job, and I said yeah. I had a pretty good-sized business. This was over in the east Texas oil field. I gave her a job. The next day, three or four women came up in the same V-8 Ford that little cross-eyed feller drove up in the day before, and they're lookin' for Jo Ann. This woman said she's gonna kill her and wanted me to fire her and all that. So I told all this to Jo Ann. That guy, his name was Webb Jay, and he's cross-eyed as he can be. Jo Ann, she always said, 'I love that little cross-eyed man.' She didn't know he's a married man.

"So, I sold that place. Later on, about two or three years later, I was sittin' in this joint over close to Longview, tryin' to get ideas for a song, and the jukebox is playin' that song of Bob Wills's, 'Take Me Back to Tulsa.' It's an eight-bar verse, eight-bar chorus, eight-bar verse, eight-bar chorus. A repetitious thing. So I said, 'I'm gonna write me a song on that same pattern.' Simple melody. Everyplace you go then, nine times out of ten the jukebox be playin' that song. It's just that old P.D. song 'Take Me Back to Texas.' So I'm sittin' there, watchin' things happen, and in came this gal Jo Ann. She's scratched up and looks like she's been fightin' wildcats. I said, 'Well, godsakes, Jo Ann, what happened?' And she said, 'Jay's old lady's after me with a gun.' I said, 'I told you to leave that married man alone, that woman gonna kill you 'bout that man.' She said, 'Yeah, but Dex'—she always called me Dex —'but Dex, I love that little cross-eyed man.' Woman had chased her about two miles through wire fences, through briars, and everything else. She was a pretty girl, 'bout eighteen, twenty years old. So I got the idea, 'Lay that pistol down, babe, lay that pistol down.' Got a woman after ya with a gun, y'know, you can't outrun the darned thing, so you gotta beg her to lay it down. So I went out to the car and started writin' these lyrics. I sang it over and over so I wouldn't forget it, and then I had my song."

Al Dexter had used an electric steel-guitarist named Bobby Simon in his first Vocalion recordings in 1936.

"Bobby, he was a Spaniard from San Antone. He was a very refined Spaniard, though. He played electric steel guitar and take-off guitar.

Al Dexter in the 1940s.

That was the first one I ever saw. It had a little bitty body and an electric pick-up on it, and he played it Spanish style. That's the one I recorded 'Honky Tonk Blues' with."

Leon McAuliffe, the best known steel-guitarist of Western swing, performed with Bob Wills from 1935 (McAuliffe was 18 then) to 1942. His first experience with an electric guitar was in Fort Worth, when Bob Dunn let the younger musician play a while with his. In the spring of 1935, Wills bought McAuliffe an amplified steel guitar. Leon admits that he was a less able artist than Dunn, who could swim farther from the constraints of melody than McAuliffe. If McAuliffe had been capable of Dunn's free-yelling style, Wills probably would not have allowed it in his music. It is hard to imagine Bob Dunn appearing as a guest soloist in the Lawrence Welk show, *Top Tunes and New Talent*, as McAuliffe did in September 1957.

After World War II, Leon McAuliffe began recording with his own band, and he continued to record by himself into the 1970s. He started with the short-lived Majestic Records, then had a Top Ten hit, "Panhandle Rag," with Columbia in 1949. After Columbia he recorded for Russell Sims's Cimarron label, Starday (some of his Starday work was reissued by Mercury), Capitol, and Stoneway. Since 1954 McAuliffe has operated radio station KAMO in Rogers, Arkansas.

Many other good steel-guitarists passed through the Texas Playboys. One of them, Noel Boggs, did the soundtrack for *War of the Worlds* in 1953.

The amplified steel guitar changed in the mid 1940s. It stood on four legs, like an insect, and had up to four separate eight-string necks. A complex system of cables, pulleys, and rods connected to foot pedals (and later knee pedals) enabled the guitarist to weirdize the pitch of individual strings and to make chords and voicings that none had heard before. The pedal steel was the invention of John Moore, a machinist and amateur musician who lived in Winsted, Connecticut. Moore worked with the Gibson company to produce the Gibson Electraharp, the first pedal steel guitar. The Bigsby company and others began manufacturing pedal steels also.

Pedal steel guitars were harder to master than conventional guitars. Men sat at this strange shining tool, their fingers gleaming with metal —doctoral, they seemed, and mystical, too. The most popular pedal steel players in the late 1940s and early '50s were Joaquin Murphy and Speedy West.

West, who was born Wesley Webb West on January 25, 1924, in Springfield, Missouri, began playing a National steel guitar about 1937. He moved to Los Angeles in June 1946, seeking work in the music business. In 1948 he bought the second pedal steel Bigsby manufactured and, that same year, worked with both Spade Cooley and Hank Penny. In the early 1950s Speedy was one of the most popular session men in L.A., recording over 6,000 records with 177 singers in five years. Many of the singers Speedy recorded with were country, but many of them were pop singers who wanted this new, mesmerizing sound in their music. In February 1952, a representative month, Speedy recorded with Rex Allen, the Bell Sisters, Jimmy Boyd, Tommy

Left to right: Speedy West, Hank Penny, Billy Hill, and Hank Caldwell.
Photo courtesy of Rich Kienzle.

Duncan, Tennessee Ernie Ford, Johnny Horton, Spike Jones, Frankie Laine, Ella Mae Morse, Tex Ritter, Fabor Robison, Billy Strange, Merle Travis, and others. (By today's standards, West was not paid too well for his session work, about $1,000 a month.)

In two 1952 recordings, Hank Thompson's "Waiting in the Lobby of Your Heart" (Capitol) and Slim Whitman's "Song of the Old Water Wheel" (Imperial), Speedy West used a bizarre, high-volume wah-wah effect that got the attention of the industry. Soon the pedal steel work heard in records coming from Nashville was louder, more emphatic than it had been. (Don Helms's pedal steel, for example, had rarely dominated the sound of Hank Williams's records.) The man who made the pedal steel the most important part of the Nashville sound was Webb Pierce (born on August 8, 1926, in West Monroe, Louisiana), one of the greatest honky-tonk singers of the 1950s.

After a handful of recordings for Pacemaker and Four-Star, Pierce signed with Decca in 1952. His first release, "Wondering," was a Top Ten hit (only one country artist, Eddy Arnold, has had more hits in his career than Pierce). He was best, and most successful, with hard-core honky-tonk stuff. "Back Street Affair," his first Number One hit, was a song of adultery. "There Stands the Glass," a hit during the winter of 1953–1954, is one of the classic booze songs and one of the strongest records of the fifties. It was released in October and very quickly banned by many stations, beginning with WXGI in Richmond, Virginia. The February 13 issue of *Billboard* reported that the record "is growing by leaps and bounds ever since the ban of the tune by many radio stations." The authors of "There Stands the Glass" wrote a sequel, "Throw Away the Glass."

There was steel in Pierce's music from the beginning, and with each record it pulsed stronger and louder. In "Wondering" the steel is barely noticeable, but for a small flourish at the end; in "That Heart Belongs to Me," Pierce's second hit, there is a full solo; in "Back Street Affair" and "That's Me Without You" the steel flows through the whole of the music; in "There Stands the Glass," the steel is the dominant instrument; in "Slowly," the biggest country hit of 1954, the steel is the force of the song. Bud Isaacs, the man who played a Bigsby steel in "Slowly," birthed the Nashville steel sound that still prevails: those dark swoonings fluid as seaweed in a bay, and often as turgid.

7 PEE WEE KING—Variety
Webb Pierce and his band visit Pee Wee King and the gang on the Cleveland jamboree. Pee Wee's other guests are singer Charlene Mills and the roller skating square dancers.

TV Guide *listing, July 25, 1955.*

When honky-tonk's popularity waned, so did Webb Pierce's. He fared well, though, and today he is a millionaire with a specially built ramp at his home to accommodate the comings and goings of tourists by the busful. Webb has a guitar-shaped swimming pool and unappreciative neighbors. During the 1976 muscular dystrophy telethon, Webb donated $100. What a sport.

Charley Ryan (born December 19, 1915, in Graceville, Minnesota) recorded a series of rockabilly records in the late fifties that used steel-guitar work to achieve a variety of weird affects. In "Hot Rod Lincoln," which he recorded on his own Souvenir label in Spokane in 1955, steel-guitarist Neal Livingston wrought sounds of speed, sirens, and whiplash behind Ryan's tough boogie beat and amphetamine vocal. Ryan had been playing, in his phrase, "country music with a beat" since about 1947. His first record, "Double Track Woman" c / w "Daddy Can I Night Herd in the Sky," was released by Keyboard in 1951. The original version of "Hot Rod Lincoln" (the flip-side was "Hank Williams Goodbye") went largely unnoticed, but when Ryan recut it for Four-Star in 1960, it became a hit in both the country and pop markets. (The previous year had seen the first steel-guitar pop hit, Santo & Johnny's "Sleep Walk.")

The original "Hot Rod Lincoln," 1955. The flip-side was "Hank Williams Goodbye."

The hit "Hot Rod Lincoln," 1960.

Charley Ryan

Instead of using pedal steel guitars, blues artists held to the older slide and bottleneck styles, increasing the volume of their amplifiers as years passed. In the late 1940s and early '50s, as the pedal steel became the major tool of country music, the electric slide was the major tool of blues, and its masters were men such as Lowell Fulson and Elmore James. (Fulson was born in 1921 in Tulsa. His grandfather was a fiddler, and the first band Fulson was in, in 1938, was Dan Wright's String Band, which played a mixture of blues, pop, and country. The group consisted of two guitars, three fiddles, two mandolins, and two banjos. Fulson began recording in 1946 and through the years has made records for Big Town, Gilt Edge, Swing Time, Aladdin, Checker, Kent, and other labels. Fulson's older records are very rare, but, like Elmore James's, they hold some of the classic and most powerful electric slide performances of the era.)

The connection between the pedal steel of country music and the electric slide guitar of blues has become very tenuous to the ear. There is an occasional clarity, as in Chuck Berry's steely "Deep Feeling," the flip-side of his 1957 hit "School Days." In 1961 Doug Quattlebaum, a blues singer born in 1927 in Florence, South Carolina, cut an album for Bluesville, *Softee Man Blues*, with a National steel guitar. But Freddie Roulette is the best example of the common stem of country and blues guitarists.

Roulette was born on May 3, 1939, in Evanston, Illinois, north of Chicago. He has recorded with blues singers such as Johnny Walker, Earl Hooker, and Charlie Musselwhite, who's white. Roulette is the first black performer since Doug Quattlebaum to cut a steel-guitar album. The album, *Sweet Funky Steel*, was released by Janus in 1973. Roulette, who plays a National eight-string, cut the album with the accompaniment of saxophones, guitar, fiddle (Sugarcane Harris), bass, and drums. One of the songs is titled "Joaquin," a tribute to Joaquin Murphey, the steel-guitarist of the 1940s. Asked of his influences, Freddie Roulette said, "Country and Western. I play steel guitar because I couldn't get out of a regular guitar what I could get out of steel."

Though he may be the last, Freddie Roulette is not the first blues performer to admit being influenced by country music. Blues singer John Jackson, born in 1924 in Rapahannock County, Virginia, has a great liking for such country artists as Jimmie Rodgers, the Delmore Brothers, and Uncle Dave Macon. Jackson was surprised when it was revealed to him that Uncle Dave Macon was white. (On October 6, 1924, Thomas Edison listened to Uncle Dave Macon's Vocalion recording of "Bile Them Cabbage Down" to decide if Uncle Dave should record for the Edison company. He made a note: "This also might do—if he is a colored man, if not they will detect it.") Jackson recorded Jimmie Rodgers's "T.B. Blues" in 1965 and the Delmore Brothers' "Gonna Lay Down My Old Guitar" in 1967. Snooks Eaglin, who was born Ford Eaglin in 1936 in New Orleans, is another blues singer who admits a liking of Jimmie Rodgers. In 1958 Eaglin recorded Rodgers's "Waiting for a Train" under the title "A Thousand Miles from Nowhere." Furry Lewis also cut "Waiting for a Train," under the title "The Dying Hobo," and attempted a yodel in it. The first stanza of "Waiting for a Train" was used by Peg Leg Howell in two records, "Broke and Hungry Blues" and "Away from Home," both cut six months after Rodgers's song.

Some of the most ancient British ballads became a part of black musical tradition in America. In the 1920s folklorist Virginia Bates of Fort Worth collected a version of "Barbara Allen" by a black woman near Hearne, Texas. In this variant, the Scotch lady Barbara Allen had become a black boy called Boberick Allen. Another black version of "Barbara Allen" was collected by Dorothy Scarborough in Virginia and included in her book *On the Trail of Negro Folk-Songs.* Scarborough also found black versions of "The Maid Freed from the Gallows," "Lord Lovel," and "Lady Isabel and the Elf-Knight," three more British ballads brought to America in the eighteenth century. "Our Goodman," the ancient song of the drunken cuckold, which surfaced in so many country records, was recorded by several blues singers: Blind Boy Fuller ("Cat Man Blues"), Coley Jones ("Drunkard's Special"), and Sonny Boy Williamson ("Wake Up Baby").

One of the earliest tellings of the enculturation of slaves to white society in America is in *The Present State of Virginia* by Hugh Jones, published in London in 1724.

> *The Negroes are not only encreased by fresh Supplies from Africa and the West India Islands, but also are very prolifick among themselves; and they that are born there talk good English, and affect our Language, Habits, and Customs.*

Writing in his journal on January 30, 1774, Philip Vickers Fithian tells of a party in Virginia. The two boys he mentions, Ben and Harry, are white.

> *This Evening the Negroes collected themselves into the School-Room, & began to play the Fiddle, & dance—I was in Mr Randolph's Room;—I went among them, Ben, & Harry were of the company—Harry was dancing with his Coat off—I dispersed them however immediately.*

In the early 1950s the Louisiana-born blues singer and harp-player Little Walter performed at a club in Dallas. The way someone described it, the scene seems not too different from that long-ago night in Virginia.

In those days they strung a rope down the center of the dance floor to keep white and colored apart, but before Walter was through that rope was down and things were right. Even the law was too hung up on the scene to keep control.

The Mississippi Sheiks, Charlie Patton, Son House, and other Mississippi blues artists derived much of their income by playing for white parties in the first part of this century; Yank Rachell and others did the same in Tennessee. Patton and Son House were received decently in white homes, and both often ate and slept in them.

Some of the most fascinating records made are those of Henry Thomas, the mysterious black singer who cut 23 sides for Vocalion in the years 1927 to 1929. He was a tramp, born in 1874 on a farm in Upshur County, Texas. His parents were freed slaves. Thomas was best known in the towns connected by the tracks of the Texas & Pacific Railroad, but he knew many other railroad routes: the Cottonbelt, the Katy, the Santa Fe, and more. There are people in Texas, old and cayman-skinned and smiling, who remember Henry Thomas—how he bragged in 1893 of his visit to the Chicago Columbian Exposition, how he bragged in 1904 of his visit to the St. Louis World's Fair, how he jumped a train to Chicago in 1927 and made phonograph records, how weeks later those phonograph records were brought to Texas by train, and how you could walk into a record store in Wichita Falls and buy them, black and lustrous and full of Henry Thomas's wild, fiery noise.

More than anyone else, Henry Thomas offers a taste of what Southern street music of the nineteenth century was like. He accompanied himself not only with guitar, but with syrinx, or Pan-pipes, which he made of bamboo. (In 1883, when Henry Thomas was nine years old, Joel Chandler Harris wrote to *The Critic* to say that, contrary to the cliches of minstrelsy, he had never seen a slave play a banjo. "I have heard them make sweet music with the quills—Pan's pipes; I have heard them play passably on the fiddle; . . . I have heard them blow a trumpet with surprising skill; but I have never seen a banjo.")

Henry Thomas's music is the oldest form of blues captured by a record company's greed. The earliest blues records, those of Mamie

Smith, Lucille Hegamin, Ethel Waters, Bessie Smith, Ma Rainey, and others who recorded between 1920 and 1925, were a very modern, sophisticated style blues: urbanely written songs set to jazz orchestrations.

The use of the word *blue* to describe an emotional state of depression or discomfort is traceable to the early sixteenth century. In the eighteenth century, the colloquialism "blue devils" referred to melancholia (the poet Burns wrote of his "blue devilism" in a 1787 letter). The first published occurrence of "the blues" was in America in 1807, when Washington Irving described "a fit of the blues" in *Salmagundi; or, the Whim-Whams and Opinions of Launcelot Langstaff, Esq., and Others.* The December 1883 issue of *Harper's* included a short story in which was written, "Come to me when you have the blues." How many songs have you heard *that* line in? (In *The Posthumous Papers of the Pickwick Club,* published in 1837, Charles Dickens used the word "funky." It is not true, however, that Philly International tried to trace Dickens's telephone number for the purpose of assigning liner notes.)

The eighteenth century, as well as the nineteenth, lingers in Henry Thomas's blues. The sound of his Pan-pipes, breezy and trilling and half-real, is the sound of an America that was the world's last blue-skied Babylon, an America that the itinerant Anglican Charles Woodmason called "low, lazy, sluttish, heathenish, hellish." He looked at the Carolina back country of the late eighteenth century as one would the griseous ass of Satan. Hear him tell of Southern women:

> *They draw their Shift as tight as possible to the Body, and pin it close, to shew the roundness of their Breasts, and slender Waists (for they are generally finely shaped) and draw their Petticoat close to their Hips to show the fineness of their Limbs—so that they might as well be in Puri Naturalibus.*

And their white trash husbands! It sickened him to see them "swopping wives as cattle." He estimated in his journal that 95 percent of the girls he married were visibly pregnant and that nine-tenths of the settlers had venereal disease. A century later this culture birthed Charlie Poole, the grandest drunk in the history of country music. The epic binge that caused Poole's death at the age of 39 on May 21, 1931, is a part of Carolina legendry.

Henry Thomas's "Red River Blues" is of a style that predates the standard verse structure of the blues. It is a blues that has not yet been tamed.

> *Which-a-way do the Red River run?*
> *Which-a-way do the Red River run?*
> *Which-a-way do the Red River run, poor boy?*
> *Which-a-way do the Red River run?*
> *Yes, she runs north and south,*
> *It runs north and south.*
> *Which-a-way do the Red River run, poor boy?*
> *Well, it runs north and south.*

His "Lovin' Babe" is closer to the blues of the twentieth century.

> *Look where the evenin' sun is gone,*
> *Look where the evenin' sun's gone,*
> *Look where that evenin' sun done gone.*
>
> *Just make me one pallet on your floor,*
> *Ah, make me a pallet on your floor,*
> *Oh, make it so your husband never know.*

The records of Henry Thomas are more than primitive blues. They are testimony of the mongrelization of black and white music. Thomas's "John Henry," "Arkansas," "The Fox and the Hounds," "Jonah in the Wilderness," "Shanty Blues," and "When the Train Comes Along" were all recorded by Uncle Dave Macon, most of them earlier in the decade. His "Charmin' Betsy" was also recorded by Fiddlin' John Carson and the Georgia banjo-player Land Norris; both recordings predate Thomas's. "Fishing Blues" was later cut by Opry star Lew Childre. "Old Country Stomp" seems echoic of the sort of party Philip Vickers Fithian described a century before Thomas's birth.

No one knows what became of Henry Thomas. Mack McCormack, a consultant to the Smithsonian Institution, thinks he encountered Thomas in Houston one afternoon in 1949. He recalls that Thomas stood about 6 feet 3 inches and that he wore several layers of clothes (McCormack counted three overcoats). By now Henry Thomas is buried, and with him an ocean of tales. In 1974 Herwin Records of Glen Cove, New York, produced an album of his complete recorded works.

The ballad of "Frankie and Johnny" is common to blacks and whites, but it originated among blacks in 1899. Allen Britt shot Frankie Baker of 212 Targee Street in St. Louis on October 15, 1899. The song was written by Mammy Lou, a singer at Babe Conner's cabaret in St Louis. In the 1920s the song was recorded by blues singer Mississippi John Hurt and by country singers such as Jimmie Rodgers, Charlie Poole ("Leaving Home"), and Darby and Tarlton ("Frankie Dean"); it was also recorded by pop bands.

"Casey Jones," a ballad associated with whites, was written by a black man. Casey Jones (born Jonathan Luther Jones on March 14, 1863, in Kentucky) was killed at 3:52 A.M., April 30, 1900, when he ran the Illinois Central Train No. 1, of which he was engineer, into the rear of a freight train near the Vaughan, Mississippi, railroad station. Wallace Saunders, a black engine-wiper at the Canton, Mississippi, roundhouse, wrote the song a few days later. It was recorded in the 1920s by both Fiddlin' John Carson and Furry Lewis.

Furry Lewis's 1928 "Kassie Jones" held an intriguing couplet.

Had it written on the back of my shirt:
Natural-born eastman, don't have to work.

Twenty years before, when there were neither blues records nor country records, folklorist Howard W. Odum collected a song that was later published in the 1925 book he wrote with Guy B. Johnson, *The Negro and His Songs.*

I got it writ on de tail o' my shirt:
I'm a natu'el-bohn eastman, don't have to work.

207

In Jimmie Rodgers's "Blue Yodel No. 9," recorded in 1930, the same couplet appears, with slight changes (Rodgers is not a natural-born eastman, but a Tennessee hustler). Gene Autry uses the couplet in his 1931 "Do Right Daddy Blues." Autry is neither a natural-born eastman nor a Tennessee hustler, but, as expected, a do-right daddy. Although it did not contain the couplet, Jimmie Davis's 1934 "Shirt Tail Blues" paid hip, oblique homage to it with its title. In 1951 Harmonica Frank Floyd cut "Rockin' Chair Daddy" for Sun. Harmonica Frank derived much of his song from "Blue Yodel No. 9," including:

> *Rockin' chair daddy don't have to work,*
> *I told her my name was on the tail of my shirt.*

The couplet surfaced in Waylon Jennings's 1975 recording of "Waymore's Blues." Waylon is neither a natural-born eastman, a Tennessee hustler, a do-right daddy, nor a rockin' chair daddy, but, simply, no ordinary dude. Last seen, the couplet drifted by in Mel Tillis's 1976 hit "Good Woman Blues." *Panta rei,* indeed.

Hear Buck Owens's 1971 hit "Rollin' in My Sweet Baby's Arms." (When the bluegrass group Country Gazette appeared in *Hee Haw* that year, they intended to perform this same song. They ran through it before the taping, and Buck Owens told them the song was too risqué, that they should perform something else. They did, and Buck had a hit.) Flatt and Scruggs recorded "Roll in My Sweet Baby's Arms" in 1950 for Mercury. In 1931 it was recorded as "I'll Roll in My Sweet Baby's Arms" by Buster Carter and Preston Young for Columbia. Carter copyrighted the song on October 9, 1931. A similar song had been collected earlier. In his 1932 book, *Episodes in Black and White,* Francis Goodwin printed a verse he had heard sung by a black man in Alabama.

> *I gwine ter lar roun' town twell de sun go down,*
> *Den it doan do me no harm, fer to roll in my*
> *honey's arm.*

Robert W. Gordon edited a column, "Old Songs That Men Have Sung," that was published in *Adventure* from 1923 to 1927. In his column of January 10, 1924, he printed a stanza sent to him by a reader who had heard it sung by blacks in railroad construction camps of the South.

> *I ain't goin' to work on the railroad,*
> *I ain't goin' to work on the farm;*
> *I'll lay round town till the pay-train comes,*
> *And roll in my Dony's arms.*

In *The Negro and His Songs*, Odum and Johnson printed a couplet similar to a verse of "Roll in My Sweet Baby's Arms."

> *Where were you las' night when I was sick in bed?*
> *Down town wid some other gal, wusn't here to hole*
> *my head.*

The first recorded use of the standard 12-bar blues style by a country singer was "James Alley Blues," recorded for Victor on March 3, 1927, by Richard (Rabbit) Brown, a New Orleans performer. It is one of the most intriguing, and least mimetic, white blues.

> *Sometimes I think that you too sweet to die,*
> *Sometimes I think that you too sweet to die,*
> *And another time I think you oughta be buried alive.* *

"James Alley Blues" was recorded six months before Jimmie Rodgers's first session, and eight months before his first blues-styled recording ("Blue Yodel," November 30, 1927).

The most powerful white blues of the 1920s is "Country Blues," cut in 1928 for Brunswick by Dock Boggs (1898–1971). It is a sere, droning thing, moanful and mean, too, pulled from more ancient songs, black and white.

All around this old jailhouse is hainted,
  good people,
Forty dollars won't pay my fine.
Corn whiskey has surrounded my body, poor boy,
Pretty women is a-troublin' my mind. **

Boggs later cut two songs that are almost identical to "Country Blues": "Sugar Baby" for Brunswick and "Old Rub Alcohol Blues" for Lonesome Ace. "Wild Bill Jones," recorded by James Luther Dickinson in 1971 and included in his Atlantic album, *Dixie Fried*, is a dark, galeforce reworking of some ancient Southern lyrics; a verse of "Country Blues" is worked in beautifully. *Dixie Fried* is one of the most bizarrely powerful musics of this century: a loud, moralless baptism of rhythm. There are the Night Caps' "Wine," Carl Perkins's "Dixie Fried," warm, visceral graftings of Dock Boggs and a thousand more drunken voices of an older, more tenebrious South, and a prowling, surly version of Bob Dylan's "John Brown" that wields an unfriendly mirror at its author's eyes.

Black blood flows in the music of Jimmie Rodgers and Cliff Carlisle; it was in Gene Autry's and Jimmie Davis's, too, before they went pop in the late 1930s. It has been suggested, strongly, that Davis often bought songs outright from black men, but the former governor said this was not true when he was asked about it by Doug Green, oral historian of the Country Music Foundation in Nashville. There is also black blood in the music of less bluesy country singers.

"Hesitation Blues" was recorded by Reaves White County Ramblers (1927), Milton Brown and His Musical Brownies (1936), and Hank Penny and His Radio Cowboys (1939). Lyrics from "Hesitation Blues" surfaced in Charlie Poole's "If the River Was Whiskey" (Poole also recorded Handy's "Beale Street Blues," under the title "Rambling Blues"), and Fiddlin' John Carson's "Whatcha Gonna Do When Your

---

*"James Alley Blues" by Richard Brown. Copyright © 1927 by Peer International Corporation. Copyright renewed. Used by permission.
**"Country Blues" by Dock Boggs. Copyright © 1966 by Stormking Music Inc. All rights reserved. Used by permission.

Licker Gives Out," which was derived from "Crawdad Song." (One of Fiddlin' John's songs, "It's a Shame To Whip Your Wife on Sunday," later turned up in a Leadbelly record.) Copyrighted by W. C. Handy in 1915 as "The Hesitating Blues," the song is related to an older black song, "Honey Take a Whiff on Me." Charlie Poole cut a variant of this, "Take a Drink on Me."

Dick Justice, a West Virginia singer who recorded for Brunswick in the late 1920s, cut Luke Jordan's "Cocaine," Bayless Rose's "Black Dog Blues," and "Brownskin Blues," derived from Blind Lemon Jefferson's songs "Dark Horse Blues" and "Stocking Feet Blues."

Blind Lemon Jefferson's "Matchbox Blues," recorded for Okeh in March 1927, was done by Kentucky mandolinist and miner Larry Hensley (1934), Joe Shelton (1935), Roy Shaffer (1939), Roy Newman and His Boys (1939), Carl Perkins (1957), and Jerry Lee Lewis (1958). Lines from the song were used by Jimmie Davis in "High Behind Blues" (1932). The essence of the song's lyrics did not originate with Blind Lemon Jefferson, but with Ma Rainey's 1924 record "Lost Wandering Blues."

> *Lord, I stand here wondering,*
> *Will a matchbox hold my clothes?*

Some country artists found themselves in the race section of record company catalogues, and were not pleased by it. The Allen Brothers (Austin Ambrose Allen, born February 7, 1901, and Lee William Allen, born June 1, 1906, both in Sewanee, Tennessee) made their first records for Columbia on April 7, 1927; they recorded for Victor from October 1928 to May 1931. Their version of the old Papa Charlie Jackson song "Salty Dog Blues," cut at their first session, was issued by Columbia in its 14000 race series instead of its 15000 hillbilly series. The Allen Brothers filed suit for $250,000, but the suit was dropped before it came to litigation. (In the 1950s Maudie Bowen, a white lady, won a libel suit against the Anderson, South Carolina, *Daily Mail,* which had mistakenly published an item about Mrs. Bowen in its Negro News section. There are other cases like this one, and this is why newspapers do not often refer to a person's race unless it's pertinent.) The Allen Brothers recorded more black-derived songs, such as Alec Johnson's "Maybe Next Week Sometime." When their recording careers ended in 1934, Austin became a singing waiter in New York, and Lee became an electrician in Tennessee. Austin also became an electrician in the 1940s. He died on January 5, 1959, in Williamston, South Carolina. Lee Allen lives in Lebanon, Tennessee.

The Oklahoma Blue Ridge Playboys agreed to have some of their records, such as "Cross Tie Blues" and "Pouring Down Blues" (both of 1930), released in a race series, but they used the name Buster and Jack for these releases.

Western-swing bands of the 1930s and '40s used a lot of black material, but not in such a vivid manner as the older country artists. The black music Bob Wills chose to perform was often effete. At the first two Texas Playboys sessions, on September 23 and 24, 1935, Wills and his band recorded twenty songs. Twelve of these were Tin Pan Alley songs or standard jazz pieces from the previous decade, four were original compositions, three were old country songs, and one was a fairly contemporary blues (Big Bill Broonzy's "I Can't Be Satisfied"). Overall, it was old stuff: "I Can't Give You Anything But Love" was a hit in 1928 (three years after Wills cut it, Katherine Hepburn sang it in *Bringing Up Baby*). "Four or Five Times" was copyrighted in April 1927 and was a hit for Jimmie Noone's Apex Club Orchestra, McKinney's Cotton Pickers, and other bands in 1928; Milton Brown had cut the song in April 1934. "Mexicali Rose" was a hit in 1923. "Wang Wang Blues" was a hit for Paul Whiteman in 1921 (one of the song's authors, Henry Busse, played trumpet in Whiteman's orchestra). "I Ain't Got Nobody" was copyrighted in February 1916. "St. Louis Blues" was a hit in 1914; Milton Brown had recorded it in January 1935 (even Guy Lombardo and His Royal Canadians had cut it). "Sitting on Top of the World," recorded by the Mississippi Sheiks in February 1930, had already been recorded by three country acts: Joe Evans (1931), Leon's Lone Star Cowboys (1932), and Milton Brown (1934).

It was uncommon for Wills to record anything of modern origin that he and the Playboys did not compose. A 1937 recording of Jimmie Lunceford's 1934 hit "White Heat" is as close as Wills came to recording the music of his contemporaries.

"Brain Cloudy Blues," recorded in 1946, includes a good deal of Kokomo Arnold's first record, "Milk Cow Blues," of 1935, which includes a good deal of Sleepy John Estes's 1930 recording of the same name; and there were three other cuts of "Milk Cow Blues" between those of Estes and Arnold: Big Bill Broonzy's (1934), Tampa Red's (1935), and the Birmingham Serenaders' (1935). Cliff Bruner's Texas Wanderers were the first country band to cut it, in 1936. In 1938 Bob Crosby's Bob Cats recorded an instrumental version, and in 1941 Johnnie Lee Wills, Bob's brother, recorded it. Johnnie Lee had never heard any of the blues versions and was introduced to the song by Cotton Thompson, a member of the band. Thompson sang in Johnnie Lee's record, and it sold well. In 1974 Johnnie Lee Wills said of "Milk Cow Blues," "I was the first one ever recorded that." Bob Wills finally cut "Milk Cow Blues" in 1969. Henry C. Speir (1895–1972), the Mississippi-born talent scout for Paramount and other record companies, held that he helped Kokomo Arnold write "Milk Cow Blues."

A general admission ticket to the 1940 Tulsa Stampede: 56¢.

Other Western-swing bands were more imaginative than Wills in their use of black music. Milton Brown and His Musical Brownies covered Tampa Red's 1934 "Somebody's Been Using That Thing," a descendant of his 1928 "Tight like That." Jimmie Revard and His Oklahoma Playboys cut the ancient "Blues in the Bottle" (another country band, Prince Albert Hunt's Texas Ramblers, recorded the blowsiest, most beautiful version of this song in 1928).

Luis Russell was a jazz pianist, writer, and bandleader, born in Careening Clay, Panama, on August 6, 1902. He began working in 1917 as a piano-player in a silent-film theater. In 1919 he won $3,000 in a lottery and moved with his mother and sister to New Orleans, where he joined the Arnold DuPas Orchestra at the Cadillac Club. In 1926 Russell's Hot Six made their first records. He changed the name of his group, and its size, regularly: Luis Russell's Heebie Jeebie Stompers, Luis Russell and His Burning Eight, Luis and His Ginger Snaps, Luis and His Orchestra. In 1934 Russell made his last recordings. He worked as a chauffeur in New York City in the early 1960s and died there on December 11, 1963.

Luis Russell was crazy, and great. On January 15, 1929, he recorded a song for Okeh titled "The Call of the Freaks," a macabre, funereal thing without words, composed by Russell's drummer Paul Barbarin. On September 6, 1929, Russell recorded "The New Call of the Freaks." It was essentially the same song, except for a ghostly, drunken chanting that rose at its end.

> *Stick out your can, here comes the garbage man.*
>   *In the mornin'.*
> *Stick out your can, here comes the garbage man.*
>   *In the evenin'.*
> *Stick out your can, here comes the garbage man.* *

The record ended with a fade-out effect, the world's first. It all seemed satanic, but very funny.

From somewhere Milton Brown and His Musical Brownies got "The New Call of the Freaks" and cut it under the title "Garbage Man Blues" at their first session, on April 4, 1934. It was faster, and those jittery, eldritch words were babbled-sung throughout. To hear "Garbage Man Blues" is to feel the space between Bob Wills and Milton

*"The Call of the Freaks" by Luis Russell and Paul Barbarin. Copyright © 1929 by Edwin H. Morris & Company, Inc. Copyright renewed. Used by permission.

Brown. Roy Newman and His Boys covered "Garbage Man Blues" for Vocalion in 1935.

Country music's last transfusion of nigger blood came in the days of rock-and-roll. Ernest Tubb cut "Kansas City Blues" for Decca in 1954;

that same year, Leon McAuliffe covered the Chords' "Sh'Boom" for Columbia. Bull Moose Jackson's 1947 "I Want a Bowlegged Woman" was cut by Jimmy Ballard on King. The Dominoes' 1951 hymn to duji-dick, "Sixty Minute Man," was cut by Hardrock Gunter & Roberta

Lee (Decca), the York Brothers (King), and, of course, Jerry Lee Lewis (Sun). (These were the sort of songs that caused headlines such as "Urge Cleanup on Smut Songs," which *Variety* yelled on November 3, 1954.) Bill Haley turned Guitar Slim's "Later for You Baby" into his 1955 "See You Later Alligator," the biggest hit of his career. Mac Wiseman cut the Clovers' "One Mint Julep" in 1956.

It also might be argued that R&B singer Wilbert Harrison turned country singer Denver Darling's "Juke Joint Mama" into "Kansas City," one of the biggest hits of 1959. (A few years earlier, Harrison had covered Terry Fell's 1954 country hit, "Don't Drop It.") Denver Darling (his real name!), born in Illinois, specialized in World War II hate songs. "Cowards Over Pearl Harbor," "We're Gonna Have To Slap the Dirty Little Jap," "Mussolini's Letter to Hitler," "The Devil and Mr. Hitler," "I'm a Pris'ner of War," and "When Mussolini Laid His Pistol Down" are some of the titles he recorded for Decca. Bob Wills cut a handful of World War II songs, including three Darling wrote: "Stars and Stripes on Iwo Jima," "Empty Chair at the Christmas Table," and "White Cross on Okinawa." Cliff Bruner made only one statement on the subject: "Draft Board Blues."

Wilbert Harrison was not the only R&B artist to look toward country music. "Tennessee Waltz" was cut by Stick McGhee (1950), Bobby

Denver Darling

Comstock (1959), and Daddy Stovepipe (1960). Darrell Glenn cut "Crying in the Chapel," which was written by his father, for Valley in

Darrell Glenn, 1955.

*The original
"Crying in the Chapel."*

the summer of 1953. Rex Allen covered it for Decca and got a Top Ten country hit, but an even better-known cover is that of the Orioles for Jubilee, the biggest R&B hit of the year. Wynonie Harris's 1951 hit "Bloodshot Eyes" was a cover of Hank Penny's Western-swing recording of the year before. Harrison cut two other country songs: Moon Mullican's "Triflin' Woman Blues" and Louie Innis's "Good Morning, Judge."

*The original
"Bloodshot Eyes."*

*Wynonie Harris's R&B hit version
of "Bloodshot Eyes."*

Harris's version was better than the original, and one of the consummate records of his career. The song fit his persona well. It is a cruel and funny song; very sexy, very unromantic, and very liquorish. Harris was the greatest of the jump blues singers, a lord of excess from Omaha, Nebraska. ("Wynonie was a mess, man," said musician Melvin Moore. "All he wanted to do was rock 'em and roll 'em.") He recorded from 1944, when he sang with Lucky Millinder and His Orchestra, to 1964, for many labels: Philo, Aladdin, Bullet, King, Apollo, Atco, Roulette, and more. His biggest hit was the 1949 "All She Wants To Do Is Rock" (King). When Wynonie realized he was dying, he called all his friends together for a wild, drunken bash. He died in Oakland in the summer of 1969, rocking to the end.

Wynonie Harris

Several of Jimmie Rodgers's songs have been cut by black artists. The Memphis Sheiks did "He's in the Jailhouse Now" for Victor in 1930; Fats Domino cut "Waiting for a Train" under the title "Helping Hand" for Imperial in 1955; Memphis Slim did a version of "T for Texas" for Folkways in 1960.

WAYNE RANEY

Bull Moose Jackson covered Wayne Raney's 1949 "Why Don't You Haul Off and Love Me" and Moon Mullican's 1951 "Cherokee Boogie." Ivory Joe Hunter covered "Jealous Heart," Al Morgan's 1949 country hit. Louis Jordan covered Tex Williams's 1950 "Tamburitza Boogie." Ray Charles cut Bob Wills's "Roly Poly" in 1952. Earl Hooker cut "Steel Guitar Rag" and "Red River Valley" in 1953, and Ernest Tubb's "Walkin' the Floor over You" in the late sixties. Eddy Arnold's 1947 hit "It's a Sin" was cut by Tarheel Slim and Little Ann in 1961. Hank Williams's songs were cut by many R&B acts, such as the Pearls ("Your Cheatin' Heart"), Bobby Comstock ("Jambalaya"), and Fats Domino ("Jambalaya"). Big Bill Broonzy cut "Sixteen Tons" in 1956. Junior Parker cut Willie Nelson's "Funny How Time Slips Away" in 1972. Ray Charles's best-selling album was *Modern Sounds in Country & Western Music*, which included Jimmie Davis's "You Are My Sunshine" (how many R&B versions of *that* are there?) and Ted Daffan's "Born To Lose." Charles's 1959 version of Hank Snow's "I'm Movin' On" was the source of the Rolling Stones's song. He recorded two more country albums, in 1962 and 1965. Esther Phillips cut a country album for Lenox in 1963 (reissued by Atlantic in 1966); the Supremes, for Motown in 1965; Joe Tex, for Atlantic in 1968; and Bobby Blue Bland, for ABC in 1975 (the much awaited and discussed Bobby Bland and George Jones duet album has still not occurred, however).

The first country artist to record with a black musician was Jimmie Rodgers, who used Louis Armstrong on cornet in his July 16, 1930, recording of "Blue Yodel No. 9." This was Armstrong's first session after moving to California earlier in the summer, and when asked about it later in his life, he could not recall the circumstances that led to it. The unidentified pianist in the record is surely not Earl Hines or Lil Armstrong, contrary to what has been said and written. In 1970 Louis Armstrong, by then a pop act, cut a fake country album. Someone asked him if it were a change of direction, and he said, "I was doing that same kind of work forty years ago."

Jimmie Davis was the second country singer to record with black accompaniment. On February 8, 1932, he cut four songs in Dallas with blues singer and steel-guitarist Oscar Woods. (Davis had first used a steel-guitarist, Snoozer Quinn, at his May 26, 1931, session in Charlotte.) Woods, like Davis, lived in Shreveport, and it seems the two men were very close. Davis arranged for Woods and his friend Ed Schaffer to cut a record the same day as his own session; this record, "Nok-'Em-All Blues" c/w "Flying Crow Blues," was released under the name Eddie and Oscar. Woods and Schaffer had recorded once before for Victor, as the Shreveport Home Wreckers. This session, on May 5, 1930, seems also to have been arranged by Davis, for he recorded the day before in the same city. In 1936, two years after Davis joined Decca, Woods recorded for that company under the name of the Lone Wolf. In 1937 Davis arranged for the black group Kitty Gray and Her Wampus Cats to record for ARC-BRC. The group featured Oscar Woods. In October 1940, John Lomax found Oscar Woods playing in the streets of Shreveport. That was the last he was seen.

Davis was not the first country artist to help a blues singer's career. Willie F. Narmour, the fiddler who recorded with guitarist Shell W. Smith as Narmour & Smith, got Okeh to sign Mississippi John Hurt in 1928. Narmour, Smith, and Hurt were neighbors in Carroll County, Mississippi.

In the early 1930s the Texas singer Al Dexter worked with an all-black band.

"Yeah, that was what I started out with. I had a saxophone, a piano, and drums, a bass. You see, when I started out it was hard times. The early thirties. A quarter was a quarter then. The big ones eat the little ones. I was barnstormin' around and playin' these joints and passin' the hat. I went up to the radio station, got me a little thirty-minute program. One day this little black woman came up to me and said, 'How'd you like to play at my place?' I said, 'Where is your place?' She said, 'I have the Avalon Club over here in Longview. Get yourself a little band. I'll give you two dollars a man, plus your tips, your kitty.' That sounded all right to me. I was happy to get any salary at all, y'see.

"So I went around, tried to get some white musicians to work with me; they wouldn't work with me. They wanted to play Benny Goodman stuff, that kind of music. I just wanted to sing songs, play music. So I met a nigro down there at Longview. He'd been playin' with white musicians. His name was Claude Crawford. I said, 'Claude, would you work with me?' He said, 'Yes, Mr. Al, whataya got?' So I told him and he said, 'That sounds pretty good to me, Mr. Al.' He was a great big guy, weighed two hundred and thirty pounds, and he could sure play a piano. He said, 'You don't mind playin' with colored people, do you?' And I said, 'Not a bit.' So we got a guy who used to play saxophone with Louis Jordan. Lee Siegler was his name; he come from Arkansas. Got a boy by the name of Hicks. He played guitar, and he played drums. I just kept hirin' 'em. Al Dexter and His Colored Band, all-nigro band. [Laughs.] We had 'em dancin' to death.''

Dexter never recorded with black musicians, but he planned to on one occasion.

"There was a colored guitar-player I had one time. I sold him a guitar. Boy, he could play it, I'm tellin' you the truth. He wanted me to take him in and record him some time, and I intended to, but he got killed. I can't think of his name now."

Dexter acknowledges taking "New Jelly Roll Blues," his first record, from a black source. Peg Leg Howell and His Gang cut "New Jelly Roll Blues" for Okeh in the spring of 1927. By then versions of "Jelly Roll Blues" were common.

One night in the late 1930s, Bob Wills got drunk and hired a black trumpet player in Tulsa. The next morning he fired him.

It is a very intriguing truth that Charlie Parker often made late-night music with Ray Price's band in the early 1950s. If any tapes of these sessions were made, they did not survive. Ray Price went middle-of-the-road in the sixties, but Charlie Parker had beat him to it: Hear his 1950 Mercury album *Charlie Parker with Strings.*

White musicians have been common in R&B. All the black artists who have recorded in Memphis, Muscle Shoals, and several other Southern cities since the 1950s have used mostly white musicians. Every time you hear an Otis Redding record, you're hearing a bunch of white boys.

Deford Bailey, born in 1899 in Carthage, Tennessee, was the first black Opry star. In 1928 Bailey made twice as many Opry appearances as any other artist. He recorded for Columbia in April 1927, but the records were not released. That same month, he recorded for Brunswick at two New York sessions. (Brunswick did not issue Bailey's records in its race series.) He made his last records for Victor, on October 2, 1928. Bailey ended his career in 1941. He refused an offer to play a role in *W. W. and the Dixie Dance Kings*, a 1975 movie starring Burt Reynolds; the part went to Memphis blues singer Furry Lewis. He has lived in Nashville since he moved there from Carthage in 1922.

SATURDAY'S PROGRAM.

WSM (282.8 Meters).

6:45—Dinner concert by Andrew Jackson hotel orchestra, directed by Beasley Smith (1 hour).

7:15—Bedtime story interlude (¼ hour).

8:00—Bill Barrett and Walter Leggett, fiddle and banjo (½ hour).

8:30—Theron \ Hale and daughters, Elizabeth and Mamie Ruth, fiddle and piano (½ hour).

9:00—Binkley Brothers, fiddlers (½ hour).

10:15—Miss Zena Mai Jones, popular pianist (¼ hour).

9:45—Tony Rose and his orchestra with Edward Stockman, baritone (¼ hour).

10:15—Miss ⅝ena Mai Jones, popular pianist (¼ hour).

10:30—DeFord Bailey, harmonica wizard (¼ hour).

10:45—Fields and Martin, Hawaiian guitarists (¼ hour).

WBAW (236 Meters).

6:00—Organ concert from the Capitol theater by Grace Mitchell and Leon Coles (1 hour).

WDAD (226 Meters).

Silent pending new installations

Radio listing, Nashville Banner, *November 13, 1926.*
DeFord Bailey is on at 10:30.

Charley Pride, country music's only black star since Deford Bailey, was born in Sledge, Mississippi, on March 8, 1938. He signed with RCA in 1966 and had his first hit, "Just Between You and Me," in December of that year. He made his Opry debut on January 14, 1967, and was brought back for three encores.

The first black girl singer to play the Opry was Linda Martell. She appeared there in August 1969. Plantation released an album by her, *Color Me Country.*

In 1971 Otis Williams, the former lead singer of the Charms, a black group that recorded for Rockin' and DeLuxe in the 1950s, cut a country album for Pete Drake's Stop label, *Otis Williams and the Midnight Cowboys.* "I Wanna Go Country," a single from the album, was a minor hit that spring.

COUNTRY

Well, I can see what happened to Jerry Lee,
And I want the same thing for me.

Blacks are not a common subject in country music, but they do occasionally appear. Hank Williams recorded "The Funeral" in 1949. Though credited to Fred Rose, it was derived, as were most of the Luke the Drifter records, from an earlier stage recitation. "The Funeral" speaks of a black preacher with "countenance grotesque." "Ethiopian face" is rhymed with "crushed, undyin' race." Twenty years later the Flying Burrito Brothers parodied "The Funeral," substituting a dumb hippy boy for the dead nigger baby.

"Black Diamond," recorded by both Stuart Hamblen and Hank Snow, tells of a World War II soldier injured in battle on a tropical island. He lay there, his hip shattered, till "an angel of mercy with a bone through his nose" carried him off to his cave in the hills. His face is described as one "that would've given death a scare." Hank Snow continued to perform "Black Diamond" into the seventies, not only in concert, but in TV shows as well.

The song Merle Haggard wrote after his 1969 "Okie from Mus-kogee" was "Irma Jackson," a soft tale of interracial sex. Capitol did not permit him to record the song then, but he did cut it in 1972. Billy Joe Shaver's "Black Rose," cut for Monument in 1973, was about the same thing. "I'm a White Boy" is a song Merle Haggard wrote but did not record. "I'm proud and white," wrote Merle. "Daddy's name wasn't Willie Woodrow; I wasn't born in no ghetto." Jim Mundy cut it for ABC-Dot in 1975.

In the mid 1920s the KKK label of Indianapolis, Indiana, released a series of records with titles such as "Why I Am a Klansman," "Cross in the Wildwood," "The Bright Fiery Cross," and "Wake Up America and Kluck, Kluck, Kluck." Thomas Edison listened to the records on July 24, 1924, to see if they were suitable for release on his label. He noted that "Why I Am a Klansman" had a "fair tune," but his final advice was, "Don't bother with this trash."

In the 1960s the Reb Rebel label was formed in Crowley, Louisiana. Crowley had been a recording center since the fifties, when Jay D. Miller cut sessions on Lightnin' Slim, Lazy Lester, Slim Harpo, and others, for his own Feature label and for Excello in Nashville. Miller sells Reb Rebel records in his North Parkeson Street music store. The most popular Reb Rebel artist is Johnny Rebel, whose records include "Move Them Niggers North," "Stay Away from Dixie," "Nigger, Nigger," "Some Niggers Never Die (They Just Smell That Way)," and "Nigger Hatin' Me." Another Reb Rebel artist, James Crow, has a more bluesy style than Mr. Rebel. In "Cowboys and Niggers" he sings of his travail in a deep, blowsy baritone.

> *The house next door to me*
> *Has been sold to niggers.*

About 1973 a well-known country singer whose work is often marked by an excessive poignancy recorded a song he calls "I Was Born in a One-Nigger Town," one of the best performances of his career. The record was not released.

Well, I used to think that he was black becuz
    the man was sick.
Us honkies hate them niggers cuz they got them
    big long dicks.
What a fuckin' disappointment when they trot
    you into class
And ya gotta hate your classmate for the color
    of his ass.
Oh, I was born in a one-nigger town;
The only black man that we had for miles and
    miles around.
Well, I was seventeen before I realized my fate:
What a fuckin' disadvantage when ya never learn
    to hate.

227

As to the identity of the singer, I will only say that it is not Kitty Wells.

I asked Warren Smith if he had gotten any bad reactions to "Ubangi Stomp" in 1956.

"No. Strange enough, a lot of people, they all liked it. We played a lot of dances, y'know, where there was a lot of colored people there, and they danced the devil out of it."

In the late 1960s and '70s country music and R&B still hold strong similarities. Look at the soul charts; look at the country charts. Both are dominated by records with dumb lyrics and fat, sticky orchestrations. Is there a difference between "Disco Duck" and "Convoy"? As it is writ: Everybody does it in Hawaii.

Shoot.

Yeah, But They Break
If You Sit On Them

In the seventeenth century, Savinien Cyrano de Bergerac closed his eyes and imagined a talking machine, a box of springs that spoke. Two hundred years later, in 1857, E. L. Scott de Martinville constructed and patented a mechanism that traced the ripplings of sound waves onto a hand-powered, lampblacked cylinder. He called it a phonautograph. Scott's machine could record sound waves, but it couldn't re-create them. On a laboratory work sheet of July 18, 1877, Thomas Edison noted that he had discovered the basic principle of mechanical sound re-creation. On February 19, 1878, he was granted a patent for his device, which he called a phonograph.

In April 1878, Edison took his curious machine to Washington, D.C., where he demonstrated it before the National Academy of Sciences and for Rutherford B. Hayes at the White House. Later that same month, the Edison Speaking Phonograph Company was incorporated in Norwalk, Connecticut.

On October 8, 1887, a new company, the Edison Phonograph Company, was founded in West Orange, New Jersey. That same year, the American Graphophone Company was founded in Bridgeport, Connecticut. On March 26, 1888, Jesse H. Lippincott, a young investor who desired to control the new industry, purchased the sales rights of the American Graphophone Company, and on June 28 he purchased the Edison Phonograph Company from Edison for $500,000. With his purchases, Lippincott formed the North American Phonograph Company on July 14, 1888.

Edison's 1877 phonograph. Courtesy Edison National Historic Site.

This may be the first genuine country record.

The North American Phonograph Company leased phonographs through various member companies, each of which had a territory to operate within. One of the most important of these member companies was the Columbia Phonograph Company, which covered Delaware, Maryland, and the District of Columbia. It joined the North American Phonograph Company in January 1889. This territory had previously been covered by the American Graphophone Company, so when North American began to fall in 1895, the American Graphophone Company bought up most of the Columbia stock.

When the North American Phonograph Company went into liquidation in 1896, Thomas Edison formed a new company of his own, the National Phonograph Company. Edison remained in the record business until 1929, two years before his death. He held to the end that the phonograph was his dearest invention.

In 1897 Emile Berliner formed the National Gramophone Company in Philadelphia. In 1887 Berliner had applied for a patent for flat disk records, and in 1897 the National Gramophone Company marketed the world's first disks. In 1900 Berliner ceased making records in America because of a patent infringement suit brought against him by Edison. Eventually it was ruled that Berliner's disks did not infringe on Edison's patent, but by then Berliner was financially ruined. During the trial, Berliner licensed Eldridge R. Johnson, owner of the Johnson Machine Works in Camden, New Jersey, to manufacture his disks. Johnson called his company the Consolidated Talking Machine Company. In 1901, when Berliner was acquitted in court, Johnson renamed his company the Victor Talking Machine Company. Victor was incorporated in Camden on October 3, 1901.

Victor fast became the most successful company in the industry. On December 7, 1926, Eldridge Johnson sold out to a group of New York bankers, who on January 4, 1929, merged Victor with the Radio Corporation of America (RCA), owner of the National Broadcasting Company (NBC). RCA had been formed on October 17, 1919, by American Marconi; NBC had been formed on September 9, 1926, by RCA.

In 1902 Columbia began producing disks, but also continued making cylinders until 1917. (The last cylinders were made by Edison in 1929.) Paper labels were first used in 1900; before that, titles had been carved into records like a potter's signature. It was also in 1900 that the first two-sided disks appeared, produced most likely as test pressings by Eldridge Johnson. Commercial introduction of two-sided disks was in 1904, when they were sold in Europe by the Odeon label of the General Phonograph Corporation. In 1908 Columbia and Victor started selling two-sided disks in America. (From 1904 to 1906 Columbia had marketed them experimentally on a very small scale.)

Advertisement, c. 1905

Advertisement, c. 1916.

In 1915 the General Phonograph Corporation, which was financed by the Lindstrom Company of Germany, formed the Okeh label in New York City. In 1916 the Aeolian Company, which had been making gramophones for three years, started its own label, Vocalion, also in New York City.

The Pathé-Frères Phonograph Company of Paris started its Pathé label in 1912. In 1914 Pathé began distribution in America and in 1921 formed the Perfect label in Brooklyn (the office moved to Manhattan in 1928, but the factory stayed in Brooklyn). The company was reorganized as the Pathé Phonograph and Radio Corporation in 1922.

The Cameo Record Corporation was started in 1922 in New York City. Cameo formed the Lincoln label in 1924 and the Romeo and Variety labels in 1926. In 1927 J. McPherson bought both Cameo and Pathé, and formed Cameo-Pathé.

The Plaza Music Company was formed in 1923 in New York City. Plaza took control of two labels the Emerson Phonograph Company (founded in 1916 in New York City) had operated, Banner and Regal. Introduced by Emerson in 1921, Regal was the first of the budget-line labels: a Regal disk cost fifty cents, while most other pop records in 1921 cost eighty-five cents or more. This brought about a price war that raged for 20 years. In the fall of 1936, Sears Roebuck was selling records on its Conqueror label at the price of six for fifty-five cents.

In August of 1929, Cameo-Pathé and the Plaza Music Company merged with the Scranton Button Company, operator of an independent record-pressing plant. This was the birth of the American Record Corporation (ARC). At the time of the merger, Cameo-Pathé had the Cameo, Lincoln, Pathé, Perfect, Romeo, and Variety labels, and Plaza had the Banner, Domino, Jewel, Oriole, and Regal labels. Some of these labels had strict retail markets, such as Oriole, which sold only at McCrory's stores, and Romeo, which sold only at S. H. Kress stores. (Dime-store labels were common in the late 1920s and 1930s. Most of them were discontinued in 1938, but Conqueror, which started in 1929 as the Sears Roebuck label for ARC recordings, lasted till 1942.)

ARC withdrew the Lincoln label in 1929, and Cameo followed in 1930. ARC also added labels, such as Broadway, acquired from Paramount in 1930 (Paramount, founded in 1917 by the New York Recording Laboratories, had formed Broadway as a budget label in 1926; an older Broadway label had existed since 1924), and the Sears Roebuck label, Conqueror.

With its many small labels, ARC created a whirl of pop, jazz, blues,

Fiddlin' John Carson's first record, 1923.

country, and sacred noise. A single recording was often released on several labels. For example, on January 13, 1930, in New York City, the Dorsey Brothers' Orchestra recorded "Have a Little Faith in Me" for ARC, and it was released on Banner, Broadway, Cameo, Conqueror, Domino, Jewel, Oriole, Perfect, Regal, and Romeo; plus two Australian labels, Clifford and Australian Vocalion; and a British label, Imperial.

In October 1930, Consolidated Film Industries, Inc. bought ARC. In December 1931, this same company bought the Brunswick Record Corporation (BRC) from Warner Brothers Pictures, who had bought it in April 1930 from the Brunswick-Balke-Collender Company of Chicago. (This is the same Brunswick, founded as a billiards manufacturer in 1845 in Cincinnati, and merged in 1879, that is familiar to devotees of *Bowling for Dollars*.) BRC's Brunswick label, formed in 1920, was an important producer of race and hillbilly records. The Brunswick 100 series, Songs from Dixie, was started in April 1927 and, at the time of BRC's sale to Consolidated Film Industries, had released sides by Deford Bailey, Dr. Humphrey Bates and His Possum Hunters, Dock Boggs, Dick Justice, Buell Kazee, the Kessinger Brothers, Bradley Kincaid, Bascom Lamar Lunsford, Uncle Dave Macon, and others. (The series continued to March 1933.) BRC had also taken over the Vocalion label in 1925. The BRC budget label, Melotone, was formed in 1930.

Broadway comes to the Opry house, April 1932.

Early in 1926 English Columbia, which Columbia had operated since 1922, bought a controlling interest in the parent company. In December 1931, English Columbia sold the American company to Grigsby-Grunow, which had grown rich from its manufacture of Majestic radios. But three years later Grigsby-Grunow went into liquidation, and, late in 1934, the BRC division of Consolidated Film Industries' ARC-BRC conglomerate purchased the Columbia Phonograph Company. The Columbia purchase included the Okeh label, which Columbia had taken over from the General Phonograph Corporation in October 1926.

On December 17, 1938, the Columbia Broadcasting System (CBS)

PLAN NOW
TO SPONSOR A GENUINE
Barn Dance Party
HILL BILLY DANCE
COTILLION - RUBE FROLIC
———•———
MAKE MONEY
FOR YOUR

Mr. Guy Colby, the Popular WLS Barn Dance Caller

LODGE - CLUB - GROUP or CIVIC ORGANIZATION IMPROVE YOUR HOUSE PARTY

If you are within 150 miles of Chicago and want a real money maker—something different that will pull a crowd—plan now to have a genuine Barn Dance party or frolic. Give your community an old-time dance they will never forget.

I know how. Let me tell you what my years of experience as an instructor of square dances, Schottisch, Polka, Herr Schmidt, Finger Tanz, Rye Waltz, Circle Two Step, March Waltz, Virginia Reel, Paul Jones, Grand March and other folk dances have taught me about personally conducting a party or dance of this kind in your community.

WRITE OR WIRE
GUY COLBY

3230 N. OCONTO AVE. or
WLS ARTISTS BUREAU   CHICAGO

Advertisement, 1937.

purchased from Consolidated Film Industries, Inc. the capital stock of ARC-BRC. This was the start of CBS's involvement in the recording industry. CBS's first move was to rename the ARC-BRC complex the Columbia Record Corporation.

The budget labels, except for Conqueror, which lingered, were dis-

Radio listing for WLS, Chicago, October 2, 1937.

continued by CBS. The ARC-BRC prestige label was Brunswick, but in 1940 CBS killed Brunswick and made Columbia its most expensive label. Vocalion, the cheaper label, was also killed, and Okeh was substituted for it.

Grand Opera at the Opry House, November 1926.

Early in 1934 Decca was formed here by English Decca. The next major company to be formed was Capitol in Los Angeles in 1942. In 1946 MGM was formed by its parent film company in Los Angeles. Mercury was founded in Chicago in 1947.

There had always been small, independent record companies (as early as June 1922, Johnny and Reb Spikes, black music-store owners in Los Angeles, formed their own "all-colored" label, Sunshine; the company only lasted for three records, the fate of many indies to come).

But beginning in the 1940s, independent record companies bloomed thick across the country.

In 1942 Ike and Bess Berman started Apollo Records in New York City, and Herman Lubinsky formed Savoy Records in Newark, New Jersey. In 1944 Bill Quinn started Gulf in Houston. In 1945 came Al Green's National Records in New York City, Sydney Nathan's King Records in Cincinnati, and three Los Angeles labels: Art Rupe's Specialty, Jules and Saul Bihari's Modern, and Eddie and Leo Mesner's Philo (which was changed to Aladdin the next year). In 1946 Jim Bulleit founded Bullet Records in Nashville, and Bill Quinn formed Gold Star to replace the Gulf label in Houston. In 1947 Leonard and Phil Chess started Aristocrat Records in Chicago (Aristocrat soon was changed to Chess), and Lew Chudd started Imperial Records in Los Angeles. In the fall of 1947 Herb Abramson and Ahmet Ertegun began Atlantic. In 1948 came Jerry Blaine's Jubilee. In 1949 Don Robey started Peacock in Houston, and Saul M. Kahl founded Freedom and Macy Lela Henry founded Macy's, both also in Houston. In 1950 Randy Wood started Dot in Gallatin, Tennessee. In 1951 Al Silver founded the Herald and Ember labels in New York City, Lester Bihari started Meteor in Memphis, and Lillian McMurry and Johnny Vincent started Trumpet in Jackson, Mississippi. In 1952 James Mattis started Duke in Memphis (Duke was soon acquired by Don Robey's Peacock in Houston), and Sam Phillips started Sun, also in Memphis. In 1953 Ernie Young formed Excello Records in Nashville as a branch of the Nashboro gospel label, George Goldner formed Rama in New York City as a subsidiary of Tico, a company that specialized in Latin music, Archie Bleyer started Cadence Records in New York City, and Vivian Carter and James Bracken started Vee-Jay Records in Chicago. These and many other independent labels had come (and, some of them, gone) by the year of Hank Williams's death, 1953.

The independents, or mongrel companies, as they were called by the major labels, often worked with products that the majors would have no part of. Theirs was, and is still, an avant-garde of economic necessity. It was not a major company that released Hank Williams's first records in 1947, but Sterling, a New York indie so ill anchored that it changed

Jailhouse Rock, 1943.

Advertisement, 1953.

its telephone number at least five times in three years. (Hank cut two sessions for Sterling: The first was on December 11, 1946, and the second on February 13, 1947.) Similarly, it wasn't a major label that issued the Beatles' first records in America, but Vee-Jay, a Chicago mongrel that released mostly R&B. (In the early 1960s other white boys had records on Vee-Jay: Ray Smith, Mac Davis, Hoyt Axton.)

Many of the indies employed mostly black artists (Chess, Vee-Jay, and so on), and some employed mostly white artists (Cadence, Dot, and so on), but the indies discovered early in the game that musical miscegenation often led to profits. Aladdin, with its great jump blues and black rock artists, also had a hillbilly series that was released on its Intro label. Savoy released not only jazz and R&B, but also country; they cut both Charlie Parker and the Texas Top Hands. King issued some of the finest R&B records of the 1940s and also some of the finest country records. Bullet recorded everyone from Owen Bradley to Milton Berle to Wynonie Harris to Bob Crosby to Sheb Wooley (Bullet's first artist) to Minnie Pearl to Cecil Gant to Jimmy Work. Jubilee cut both doo-wop records (the rarest R&B record, "Stormy Weather" by the Five Sharps, was on Jubilee; it's worth at least $2,000) and Jew comedy routines.

Things were never easy for the mongrel labels. Sometimes a hit record brought ruin to a label. It happened like this: Mongrels had no distribution systems of their own (this is what made them independent, really), and the distributors they used usually, or often, took advantage of the situation. When a record is distributed, payment for that record is not made directly to the record company, but through the distributor, which is actually the wholesale arm of the company. When an independent label had a hit, that meant many more copies of the record had to be manufactured than usual. If the hit sold a million units, the company owed whatever pressing plant it used a whole lot of money for manufacturing those million records. The income from the hit would easily have covered manufacturing costs and left a juicy profit. But often when the company went to its distributor to collect the money its million-seller had made, the response was, "What hit? It sold twenty thousand units." Most independents had neither the money nor the

GeePee
GILBERT PRODUCTIONS

Produced By:
Ralph Davis

Opulent Music
Time 2:42
(PRP 25651)

THE BOTTLE IN THE HAND
(Ronnie Mack)
MOE BANDY
And The
MAVERICKS

THUNDER
INTERNATIONAL
COLUMBIA, MISS.

Always a
BIG
SOUND

Record No:
1030
ZTSC-63880

Conrad Music
- BMI
T-30
Time: 1:41

"DIMPLES"
John Lee Hooker and J. Bracken
FELTON JARVIS

HARLEM

Riviera Music
BMI-2:55

Producer:
E. J. Henke

HM-107-1
45 RPM
LH-8636

WHY, WHY, WHY
(D. Sahm)
DOUG SAHM

HONEY CHILE
(Billy Joe Shaver)

TEXAS RECORD CO.

Pub. Co.
BMI
Time 2:33
2093
(SoN 59412)

BILLY JOE SHAVER

Texas Record Co. Waco, Texas

RAMCO
A DIVISION OF AUDIO RECORDERS OF ARIZONA, INC.

1997

Talent Town Songs
Renda Music Inc.
BMI (1:29)

ANOTHER BLUE DAY
(W. Jennings)
WAYLON JENNINGS

1830 NORTH SEVENTH STREET • PHOENIX, ARIZONA 85006

REM
RECORDS

Bayco-Fayette
Music—BMI

45-452
Time 2:50

PLAY ALL THE SAD SONGS
(Dave Coe-Betty Ford)
DAVE COE &
BETTY FORD

GULF RECORD COMPANY ★ HOUSTON, TEXAS

Gulf

NAILS IN MY COFFIN
(IRBY)

JERRY IRBY

103-A

FULL RANGE

D

Starrite
1559 - BMI

Vocal
Time: 2:10

NEW BABY FOR CHRISTMAS
(G. Jones - L. Blackwell)

GEORGE JONES

1226

TALLY

P.O. BOX 842

BAKERSFIELD, CALIF.

SING
A SAD SONG
(Wynn Stewart)

Owen Publications
(BMI)
Time: 2:25
Produced by
Fuzzy Owen
Dist. by
Fabor Records

MERLE HAGGARD

Accomp. by Wynn Stewart Orch.

T-155-A

ZERO

Sure-Fire Music
Co. Inc. (BMI)

45 RPM
(112-A)

THE DARKEST DAY
(Loretta Lynn)

LORETTA LYNN

112

SARG
Records
311 E. Davis St., Luling, Texas

Acuff-Rose
BMI - Time: 2:45

Vocal by
Little Doug Sahm
with Music by
The Bandits

A REAL AMERICAN JOE
(Little Doug Sahm - R. P. Phillips, Jr.)

LITTLE DOUG

113-45

courage (for some distributors long, long ago were tied in with The Boys) to initiate legal action. Lacking the money or the credit to cover their pressing-plant bills, the mongrel went into liquidation.

But where in this century-old pail of convolutions do the first country recordings occur? It is commonly said that the first country record made was the June 30, 1922, Victor recording "Sallie Goodin" c/w "Arkansaw Traveler" by fiddlers Eck Robertson (born Alexander Campbell Robertson on November 20, 1887, in Delaney, Arkansas) and Henry C. Gilliland (from Altus, Oklahoma, Gilliland was born, somewhere down here, about 1848). This may be the first country record by authentic country artists, but there were many earlier recordings of country songs by artists who probably had their roots in pop. Should these records be excluded from consideration because of their pop context? If yes, what of most of the records currently in the *Billboard* country charts?

Len Spenser had recorded "Arkansas Traveler" for Edison in 1902 (this recording was also issued by Victor several years later). The Victor Military Band cut "Soldier's Joy," a traditional rural fiddling tune before 1920. There were other records like these: stylized adulterations of a music that the record companies felt was not commercial in its real state. This is not too different from the way record companies treated black music before 1920. A 1917 Columbia catalogue includes several recordings of blues, but they are all performed by Prince's Band (Charles A. Prince was the musical director of Columbia), or by minstrel acts such as Collins and Harlan. A 1920 Victor catalogue has a special category: "Blue" Records. Titles include "Hesitation Blues," "Alcoholic Blues," "Kansas City Blues," "Mournin' Blues," "Dallas Blues," and others. Most of these are performed by the Victor Military Band, the rest by small pop groups such as the All Star Trio, who do a saxophone-xylophone-piano version of "Alcoholic Blues," described in the catalogue as a fox trot.

A catalogue published in the spring of 1892 by the Louisiana Phonograph Company, Ltd., of 128 Cravier Street, New Orleans, lists two groups of recordings by a man named Louis Vasnier. One is a series of black-dialect recitations called Brudder Rasmus Sermons. There are

245

seven of these, including "End ob de Worl," "Charity ob de Heart," and "Why You Are Black." The catalogue states, "These sermons, while very humorous, are characteristic Negro delineations and are faithful reproductions of a dusky style of pulpit oratory that is rapidly passing away. The sermons are very popular amongst both whites and blacks and have proved to be among the most profitable of all exhibition records." The other group is of coon songs. There are eight titles, including "Black Pickininny," "Coon with a Razor," and "Turkey in de Straw." All these songs are accompanied by banjo, the typical instrument of minstrelsy.

No one has come forward with a Louisiana Phonograph Company record, but it is not impossible that the company, located in the deep South, recorded not only coon songs, but some real country, blues, and jazz records.

Northeast Mississippi, 1953

The gun, a Ruger .22, is on the table, and it is three o'clock in the afternoon. In an hour Willis and Tommy and John will arrive, and the country singer will shoot them after they close the door behind them. Then he will put on his hat and leave. He will return to Oregon, slowly, not using the new highways. In Oregon he will call the Nashville office and ask the details of the awful, awful accident. I've been hunting, out on the Cape, he will say. I just got back this morning.

He will call Robert in L.A., then, and tell him how he shot Willis and Tommy and John. And he will demand what is rightfully his.

Everything will have been so easy. It isn't even a sin. It can't be, not when you hate them so much. And Tommy, especially him, patting my back with the smell of Louise still on his hand. Shit.

After he meets with Robert, he will take his wife to Spain, and they'll just set in the sand drinking and smoking and sleeping. And when they get back he'll go get them a television at Uneeda, like he's been promising. All of it, just a Viceroy away.

There is a knock. The country star holds the gun with both hands. "It's open."

They came in, the three of them, or maybe just the one or two. He was shot in the face. When he was found the next morning by the colored cleaning woman, there was a paper sack over his head, stuck fast and black with dried blood.

Index

INDEX